SPIRIT-EMPOWERED PRAYER

PARTNERING WITH GOD IN ADVANCING HIS KINGDOM

"Bishop Manny Carlos is a man of prayer. He has lived and walked his teaching on prayers. When he leads in prayer, it is endowed with power and anointing. I endorse and highly recommend the reading of Spirit-Empowered Prayer."

—BISHOP LEO ALCONGA

National President, Philippines For Jesus Movement
Executive Director, International Needs Philippines

"Bishop Manny Carlos anchors his teaching in God's word, in the example of Christ, and in the very present and loving work of the Holy Spirit. Sharing his ongoing prayer journey with candor and grace, he encourages all Jesus-followers to embrace the God-centered, lifelong practice of prayer."

—ELLEN L. MARMON, Ph.D.

Director, Doctor of Ministry Program
Asbury Theological Seminary

"If I were to be asked to describe Manny Carlos, my first response would be a man of prayer. For over thirty years, I have not only witnessed Manny to be a man of prayer but have been inspired to live a life of prayer. This is what excites me about this book. More than a publication, it is a testimony to life lived in prayer."

—JOEY BONIFACIO

Senior Pastor, Every Nation Singapore
Oversight Team member, Every Nation Churches & Ministries

"Manny Carlos is the Bishop of prayer. In Spirit-Empowered Prayer, Carlos centers the reader in a lifestyle of prayer that is both graceful and intentional. This book not only gives beautiful insights into the heart of personal and corporate prayer, it carries the reader into new patterns of prayer almost without trying. If you long for the kind of awakening experienced only by grace-centered communities of prayer, then read this book."

—DAVID B. WARD, Ph.D.

Author, Practicing the Preaching Life

"An impassioned plea to live out the uncommon prayer life of Jesus by communing with God in the power of the Spirit! Here is a major contribution to a theology of prayer from one of Victory and Every Nation's key leaders. Resisting formalism and legalism on the one hand, and undisciplined lives on the other, Bishop Manny grounds the practices of personal and corporate prayer (and fasting) as ways of communing with God ever more deeply through the Spirit's power, and bearing fruit in Christ's name."

—TIM GENER, Ph.D.
Chancellor and Professor of Theology
Asian Theological Seminary

"This volume from my dear friend Bishop Manny reads like a spiritual alarm clock; a call towards God's spiritual awakening. It's a call to new unplumbed depths of worship and prayer stemming from a slowed-yet-immeasurable intimacy with our God. I have seen Manny up close live these words out as a powerful prophetic mouthpiece that God has used to shape nations, while himself drawing from a deep and disciplined relationship with God. May this book help us all to turn down the volume of the noise of life, and turn up our passionate pursuit of God!"

—NELI ATIGA
Senior Pastor, Every Nation Brisbane

"The Personal Prayer Matters sections are pure gems—simple yet profound prayers that can lead you to God's presence! It is an easy guide for someone new to the prayer disciplines, yet deep enough for a seasoned intercessor to linger in and go deeper. I can't wait to give this book to my friends!"

—MARY MALINAO
Pastor and intercessor, Victory Dubai

"It is a grim reality that we live in a world that is increasingly connected in a global technological village and yet increasingly disconnected from God. That is why I believe that this book by Bishop Manny will help break open a watershed of liberating principles for a life spent in tangible communion with the living God. Realistic, authentic, and grace-centric, Spirit-Empowered Prayer accurately speaks the biblical essence of prayer to this generation. Having known Bishop Manny since his early days as a young pastor of Victory, I can say that this kind of book could only have been authored by someone like him. It is the inevitable overflow of his true love relationship with the God of our salvation."

—BRO. EDDIE C. VILLANUEVA
House Deputy Speaker for Good Governance and Moral Uprightness
18th Congress, Republic of the Philippines

"It is with great pleasure that I recommend this great book on prayer and a "Pray-er"—a great man of God named Manny Carlos who shares his own life of growth in prayer over decades of ministry. The book equips the reader in so many practical ways with the richness of an advanced seminar, yet is personal and inspiring as Bishop Manny recounts his development in pastoring and church planting. This book does not just inform; it imparts the power of the Holy Spirit for an adventure in your own life of prayer."

—PASTOR MARK BELILES, Ph.D.
President, Global Transformation Network
Director, International Networks of the Global Council of Nations

"A must-read book for all church leaders and those dreaming to serve God in the most effective ways. Written by a humble man of God whose ministry team rocked the whole country with the most relevant ways of presenting the gospel, who admitted it is not because of man's plans and wisdom, but on bended knees and faith in the faithful God who answers the prayers of those who pray fervently."

—BISHOP NOEL A. PANTOJA
National Director, Philippine Council of Evangelical Churches
President, Philippine Relief and Development Services

"I have known and worked with Manny for over thirty years. He has always been deeply spiritual, passionate about Jesus, and full of the joy of the Lord. In his years in vocational ministry, he has served as a worship leader, church planter, pastor, teacher, prophet, professor, and now the dean of spiritual life at Every Nation Seminary. I'm excited for this book because it flows from a lifetime of fruitful public ministry and private devotion. Regardless of the circumstance, his first instinct is to pray and seek God, which is why he's the best person to convict, inspire, and orient our lives toward prayer. Thank you, Bishop Manny, for living a prayerful life and inspiring us to do the same."

—DR. STEVE MURRELL

Founding pastor, Victory
President and cofounder, Every Nation Churches & Ministries

SPIRIT-EMPOWERED PRAYER

PARTNERING WITH GOD IN ADVANCING HIS KINGDOM

MANNY CARLOS

WITH WALTER WALKER

EVERY NATION
RESOURCES

Published by Every Nation Resources,
P.O. Box 1787. Brentwood, TN 37024-1787. USA.

Library of Congress Cataloging-in-Publication Data
Carlos, Manny
Spirit-Empowered Prayer: Partnering with God in Advancing His Kingdom
ISBN: 978-0-9752848-5-8

Printed in the United States of America

CONTENTS

ACKNOWLEDGMENTS

I would like to express my deepest appreciation to the following who have contributed in one way or another to the completion of this book:

Dr. Steve Murrell, my pastor, leader, and mentor who asked me to write this book, believing that it could contribute to stirring Spirit-empowered prayer in our global church-planting movement;

the Victory Bishops Council, led by Pastor Gilbert Foliente, Bishop Ferdie Cabiling, Dr. Jun Escosar, Bishop Juray Mora, and Pastor Michael Paderes—for your partnership in leading our churches in the Philippines and other nations these last three decades;

Pastor Joey Bonifacio—for your friendship all these years and example as a man of prayer and a family man; and to Pastor Jim Laffoon, my friend and mentor in the prophetic and prayer;

the Victory Quezon City (now Victory Katipunan) church planting team, Pastors Neil and Blanche Bernardino, Edgar and Jeng Gorre, and our first student leaders, Sharon Mayo, Carlos and Belle Antonio, and Jo Anne Flores, with whom I learned to apply persevering corporate prayer in birthing and establishing the congregation at the University of the Philippines Diliman campus;

Pastors Christian Flores and Raymond de Guzman, our present and immediate past Victory Katipunan senior pastors—for your shepherds' hearts for the church that my wife and I love;

our prayer group led by Pastors Jojo Henson, Joel Barrios, Mary Malinao, Jonathan Bocobo, and our faithful intercessors—for over fifteen years of consistently meeting every Wednesday morning in the Every Nation Building (except when there are typhoons and holidays) to pray for our church, our nation, and the nations;

my faithful prayer partners, Pastor Erwin Ramos, Marite Castro, Marie Plopinio, Jo Peña, Sally Ladignon, and Maj Yu—for continually praying for my family and me;

Pastor Walter Walker—for helping me with your wisdom and guidance in co-writing this book, and Varsha Daswani and Ruth Suson-Gloria—for providing accurate information concerning the history of our church and helping in the final edits;

the Every Nation Seminary faculty—for the theological sharpening and equipping of Every Nation pastors and missionaries, not only in theology but also in spirituality;

my dear wife, Mini, and children, Jeremy, Daniel, Hannah, and Samuel—for being my inspiration in serving God;

and ultimately my Father, the Lord Jesus Christ, and the Holy Spirit—for saving me and calling me with a holy calling, and reminding me that the prayer of a righteous person is powerful and effective.

FOREWORD

A book about Spirit-empowered prayer could only be written by a Spirit-empowered disciple of Christ. Bishop Manny Carlos, who has served as a pastor for over thirty years, is all that and more. He is a man of towering intellect and deep faith but also teachable and transparent with a childlike love for his heavenly Father. I've counted it a privilege to be his friend and co-laborer, having spent hundreds of hours together in meetings and ministry. As members of the Every Nation global apostolic team, I've watched Manny for over twenty-five years and can say without the slightest reservation that his life consistently demonstrates this book's central premise—that communion with God and the empowering presence of the Holy Spirit are the keys (the only keys) to genuine spiritual transformation. When it comes to the pursuit of God and intercessory prayer for the nations, Manny is the real deal.

Throughout *Spirit-Empowered Prayer*, he uses examples from the formative years of his spiritual life to make an inescapable point—that regimens and resolutions to pray more faithfully, more passionately, and more effectively are alone insufficient to sustain spiritual disciplines. His initial efforts in following various formulas of prayer echoed the early frustration of the apostle Paul in Romans 7—desiring to do one thing but lacking the power to accomplish it apart from the power of the Spirit.

Manny builds on this theme of spiritual empowerment with a description of one of his sixteenth-century heroes of the faith, Brother Lawrence of the Resurrection, whose rule of discipline was a retreat from the heavy burden of monastic rules to a full-time contemplation of the love of God and a radically simplified approach to spiritual disciplines. The chapters that follow serve as a practical guide to becoming a disciple fully engaged in a Spirit-led prayer life, one without the formalized prescriptions that promise a greater communion or the reliance on an individual's will power to overcome the power of fleshly desires. He devotes chapters to lessons he has learned about corporate prayer, cultivating the presence of God, and interceding for a great awakening. Manny gets even more practical in his discussions about how to create a culture of prayer and fasting within each local church. He also presents examples of how intercession on behalf of unbelievers became such an essential element of Victory, our church in the Philippines, and our Every Nation churches around the world.

Put simply, if you're a person hungering and thirsting for a deeper and more meaningful prayer life—one that is far more empowered by communion with God and far less dependent upon formalism or rules of discipline to sustain your devotion, then this could be the book for you. I should, however, also include this warning: Though the method is very simple, the cost is very high. It is nothing short of absolute surrender to the love of God and the desire to live continually in his presence.

Jim Laffoon
Brentwood, Tennessee
October 2021

INTRODUCTION

And the word of God continued to increase, and the number of the disciples multiplied greatly.

— ACTS 6:7

I never intended for things to turn out this way or to follow a path that has taken me so far from my originally chosen career. It happens all the time to college students and young professionals. Sometimes that's a good thing; sometimes, not so much. Being privileged with a good education not afforded to most of my countrymen, coupled with aspirations and idealism for a better nation, I was off to a good start. Having earned degrees from some of the most prestigious academic institutions of the Philippines and the United States, my objective was to become a highly successful business executive with all the perks of the corporate world. After some years, I would seek a leadership position in government and become a catalyst for change in our entrenched corrupt political system. My aspirations were self-serving yet noble. Then, I heard Jesus calling me to follow him. The carefully planned career eventually jumped off the tracks and headed into an unpredictable and uncertain direction, much to the concern of my family who had invested substantially in my future. Yes, I had my share of uncomfortable discussions with my parents as they (more than I) agonized over my decision. To them, I had traded in all my professional goals to serve Jesus.

In the early years of his ministry, Jesus invited various individuals to join him. Some responded, but others gave excuses for not heeding his call. Eventually, he appointed the seventy-two, who were to go before him to proclaim his kingdom with authority and power (Luke 10:1–24). As a

1

consequence, those who hesitated or simply chose not to follow missed history's rarest opportunity—to be a member of the seventy-two. Thanks to an insurance salesman, a childhood friend, and a couple of campus ministers at the University of the Philippines, along with some intense prayer on my behalf, I chose to follow Christ when I heard his summons. I was filled with the Holy Spirit, and my heart was on fire for his kingdom. Though I could never have imagined the radical departure from my career path, I am so thankful that I didn't miss that boat.

In the churches I attended early on in my faith journey, I had a growing desire to pray and fast. Through a series of events, I had come to believe in the power of prayer in partnering with God to see his kingdom and will being done on earth as it is in heaven, and sincerely endeavored to devote myself to the practice. Though I could make a good go of it for a while, I discovered that a consistent prayer life was hard to sustain. No matter how I mustered my determination, I could not consistently do what I wanted to do or be the person of prayer I wanted to be. When I fully surrendered my life to Christ, I just wanted to serve him in the vocational path that had been prepared for me. I didn't know at the time that I would have to give up my dreams for his greater dream for the world, to see peoples saved and nations transformed. Rather than aspire to be a business and government leader, Jesus was now calling me and my co-workers to disciple future businessmen, congressmen, and senators. Victory, our church in Metro Manila, started off as a ragtag group of teenagers and college students—certainly not high-ranking government officials. Yet we believed that God had given us the vision to change the campus and change the world.

After two decades of serving as a pastor, I was ordained as one of three bishops of a growing and ever-expanding family of churches in the Philippines that had in turn planted churches in Asia and the Middle East. Having been in ministry now for over thirty years, I also managed to finish a Doctor of Ministry degree from Asbury Theological Seminary.

As a member of the Bishops Council of Victory, my present role is to promote and advocate for prayer in our churches. I am attempting to follow the priorities of the early apostles—devoting myself to prayer and the ministry of the word amidst the many needs of the rapidly growing church in Jerusalem (Acts 6:4). I lead congregations and small groups in prayer, teach and train on prayer, and talk to God in solitude about all things that relate to the Victory congregations. Together we pray for nations and for our efforts to make disciples among them; for the sick, the poor, the oppressed, and the unbelieving; for a great spiritual awakening, for the governing authorities, and against the powers of darkness; for protection, provision, and power of the Holy Spirit to be manifest in our churches; and for countless other things—anything that concerns our heavenly Father's heart and purpose, which is everything.

I can truly say that prayer, communion, and the ministry of the word have become my prime objectives. It's where I'm headed, the path I have chosen. Perhaps better said, it's the path chosen for me. As my friend Bishop Ferdie Cabiling said so well in his book, *RUN*, this is the particular race God has set before me (Hebrews 12:1), and as I continue to run, I've gradually become stronger and better; more empowered and better equipped. Metaphorically speaking, a "twenty-kilometer prayer-time" would once have been unthinkable, but over time, and even more so since the coronavirus pandemic in 2020, I've learned about praying with endurance and about fixing my eyes on Jesus, the source and perfecter of my prayer life. I hope to be as committed to my race as Ferdie has been to his.

One of my greatest hesitations about agreeing to write a book on prayer is the conveyed assumption. It suggests that I have figured all this out, I have discovered some secret, I have mastered prayer and devotional life, or prayer and communion with God have become so easy and natural that I'm able to simply sit back and let it happen. Well, that's not even remotely the case. This is a life-long journey of following Jesus as his disciple and of learning to fellowship with the Holy Spirit as easily and unceasingly as he did. There are a hundred other topics that could be addressed and, in fact, have been published in thousands of books on prayer. I haven't set out to exhaust the topic. That would be like writing a travel guide to places I have never been. Nevertheless, the joy of knowing and walking with the triune God is what has motivated me to share the spiritual lessons on prayer that I have learned along the way. These lessons are what the following chapters are about.

CHAPTER ONE

PURSUING PRAYERS

For your name's sake, you lead me and guide me.

— PSALM 31:3

I became a believer and follower of Jesus in 1984, a year after graduating from the University of the Philippines (UP). Though it's not uncommon to hear people say that they "found Jesus" or even that "Jesus found them," I thought such comments were quite extraordinary. It never occurred to me that either one of us was lost. During my college years, members of the Campus Crusade for Christ in UP had twice tried to point out the nature of my lostness, but their *Four Spiritual Laws* presentation didn't get much traction with me. I remained aloof and rather proud of my restraint. There was, however, the temptation to launch into a defense of my religious traditions. For the first through the sixth grades, I went to an elementary school operated by the Jesuits and attended Mass regularly throughout high school and college in the village chapel where my family lived. I distinguished myself among my friends by sitting through the Mass while they sneaked outside to smoke. By virtue of those efforts, I considered myself a good enough Catholic. I was grateful for my religious upbringing and that I knew about the Father, Son, and Holy Spirit, as well as the Ten Commandments, but I was ill-equipped to defend my Roman Catholic faith. I was just fulfilling my religious duty. Nonetheless, I was slightly irked that someone who didn't even know me had the nerve to suggest I change religions. Deep down, what really bothered me was that after all those years, I had almost nothing to say about what I believed or why. So, I chose not to argue. No doubt those two UP Campus Crusade students were led by the Spirit to make what must have seemed like an unsuccessful gospel presentation. However, that conversation intrigued me for some time.

In mid-1984, I had a chance encounter in our village with a childhood friend. It had been a few years since Jet Antonio and I had seen each other. We took turns catching up on how things were going for us. It was one of those conversations in which it was hard to resist talking about the dreams and plans for all the big things you were going to accomplish. After graduation from UP, I had accepted an engineering position at a multinational oil company. I was pretty proud of that and could hardly wait for the opportunity to casually mention it. After all, I assured Jet, it was just a stepping stone to bigger and better things. My friend worked the conversation around to the topic of religion. And, of course, I responded with a comment about trying to live a good Christian life. At that point, our conversation shifted to a more serious tone.

"You know what would save you, Manny?"

I suddenly felt like I was in catechism class again, trying to think of the correct answer to the priest's question. However, this was a rhetorical question, and thankfully, Jet continued without giving me a chance to answer.

"It's by putting your faith in Christ **alone**, not in your own goodness."

He went on to quote from Paul's epistle to the Ephesians: "For by grace you have been saved through faith. And this is not your own doing; it is the gift of God, not a result of works, so that no one may boast" (Ephesians 2:8–9). When asked if I had ever heard that verse, I had to admit that I had not. Of course, that could have been said about almost any passage on what I would later come to understand as *sola fide* (by faith alone), *sola gratia* (by grace alone), and *solo Christus* (by Christ alone).

Two thoughts crossed my mind. Maybe I had overdone it with my comments about my great job and my big dreams, and Jet's comeback had to do with my thinly veiled boasting about my promising career. My second thought was that someone was after me, and if it was God, my mother must have had something to do with it. It's not that she had arranged the chance encounter meeting with Jet and certainly not the conversation with the two students at UP. While my father was an absentee Catholic, my mother was a devout Methodist and the daughter of a lay Methodist minister. Mom accepted Christ as her savior at age fifteen and was as bright of a light for Christ as anyone I had ever known. Though she would have preferred that I embraced her Methodist upbringing, she followed my father's preference that I would be brought up Catholic. My mother could not have been more gracious and never said a negative word about it. I wondered if the persecution her family experienced growing up in her home province for being a Protestant might have heightened her concern about the same thing happening to my siblings and to me. It should have been no surprise that she was still praying for me. Some of my earliest memories were of her leading me in a simple prayer each night, and I had no reason to believe she had stopped. In retrospect, my spiritual apathy during the years at UP had most likely fueled her continuing prayers for me as well as for my siblings. Just as Jacob wrestled with the angel of the Lord (Genesis 32:22–32), my mom was persistently wrestling with the Lord over her spiritually apathetic son. From this conversation, the reality of the power of prayer eventually dawned on me in a somewhat unexpected way. I began to realize that God was after me, and it would only be a matter of time before the next evangelist showed up.

· · ·

It was a few months after my chance encounter with Jet that my immediate boss at the oil company, Chito Poblete, came into my office and introduced me to his insurance agent. Chito had just recently surrendered his life to Jesus. It was another divinely orchestrated ambush. The quick introduction and discussion about religion turned into a conversation about being born again. It was the first time I had ever heard the phrase, and I was as bewildered as Nicodemus at his first encounter with Jesus (John 3:1–8). My assumption was that I was born and baptized into the church, and that was quite sufficient. Perhaps the term "sufficient" is not the best descriptor. As awakening teenagers, prone to wander into trouble, the catechists would often remind us that salvation was dependent on a lot of things. And it was important to keep up the good works because none but the saints (most of whom were already dead) and a few of the ultra-holy could be sure of their eternal outcomes. The idea of the **sufficiency** of Christ's sacrifice and the **assurance** of salvation was completely foreign to my way of thinking. It seemed too good to be true. I was struck by the simplicity and clarity of the insurance agent's gospel presentation.

The English poet, Francis Thompson (1859–1907), referred to the pursuing Holy Spirit as "the hound of heaven," and it was obvious that he was drawing me closer to himself. Being pursued by the Holy Spirit, I felt like the man who frequently went out onto the lake in his boat because he had heard stories about this mythological creature called a fish. He'd never actually seen a fish, much less caught one. He would return each week because he enjoyed the people of the village, the stories they told, and the songs they sang about the great monster in the lake. He also continued the habit of dropping the hook into the water because that was what everyone else did. Then one day he was shocked to discover that something was alive and on his line, pulling him into the deep and perilous waters. The monster was real after all!

That was a little like what it was for me. I'd attended church most of my life, religiously dropping my unbaited hook in the water with no real expectation of catching anything. Then to my astonishment, suddenly something big and powerful was on my line. Right there in my office, I prayed to receive Christ into my life, repented of my sins, and put my trust in his sacrifice alone for my salvation. I felt a heavy weight had been lifted from my soul, and something (or someone) came alive within me. Immediately, I was hungering and thirsting for more.

I had never really believed that God paid much attention to my prayers, and even if he was aware, what difference would it make? During the times that I did pray, I was merely reciting the scripted responses in church. But mom's prayers—that was different, and now something was different inside me as well. I started attending Bible studies at work where my boss was a participant. When the study leaders laid their hands on me and prayed for me to receive the baptism of the Holy Spirit, I immediately began speaking in unknown tongues. I was alive in Christ. I sensed an overwhelming joy from being filled with the Holy Spirit, and I had the assurance (I knew that I knew) that Jesus Christ was my Savior. No doubt there were still a lot of weeds and thorns trying to choke out the seed that had been planted in my heart. I needed to be discipled, which would come a little later.

Attending Bible study and being baptized in the Holy Spirit, I began to slowly develop the confidence to pray conversational prayers with God. It was amazing that I could actually talk to God as a son talks to his parents. Christianity offered a relationship with God, opened for us through Christ's death and resurrection, not just a set of moral imperatives to follow. Over time I discovered that the Scriptures provided a vocabulary by which I could petition the Father for things that I needed and the situations I faced. After two years with the company, doors began to open that would lead me along a rather circuitous route, eventually delivering me to the doorstep of Victory in Metro Manila. The three-year journey began with a side trip to the United States.

• • •

The mid-1980s was a period of political upheaval and economic turmoil in the Philippines, brought on by the assassination of former Philippine senator Benigno Aquino Jr. on August 21, 1983, on the tarmac of Manila International Airport. The government came under siege by student radicals from the University Belt (U-Belt) and other campuses of Metro Manila. In July 1984, amid riots in U-Belt, Pastor Steve Murrell, Pastor Rice Broocks, and a team of sixty American short-term missionaries came to the Philippines to preach the gospel and reach students. That led to establishing Victory in the basement of the Tandem Cinema. If I had been planning my life, I would have been led by an unseen hand to U-Belt and the American team. How I would have loved being a part of those early days! But God had other plans.

By Filipino standards, our family was considered upper middle class, but up to this point, all my high school and college education had been covered by academic scholarships. My mother was promoted in 1984 to become an officer at an international development bank based in Manila, a position that provided her and our family with the resources to fund continuing education for my other siblings and me. My parents began to talk to me about furthering my education in the United States. Though they never explicitly stated their concerns, the instability of the economy and the government in the Philippines probably had much to do with their suggestion. Since a master's degree for engineering graduates usually lands one in a management position, I began applying to the MBA programs of several prestigious business schools in the US, which eventually led to my admission at the Darden School of Business of the University of Virginia (UVA). Located in Charlottesville, UVA was founded in 1819 by Thomas Jefferson, the author of America's Declaration of Independence.

In 1985, my first year at UVA, I attended a Presbyterian church, which helped me get back into listening to God's word in the midst of academic pressures and homesickness. At the end of the second semester, I was able to get a three-month summer internship with a major food company in White Plains, New York, where I got connected with a small New Testament church community. This is where my faith was revived through their charismatic worship and practice of spiritual gifts. It was also there that I finally got water baptized. With my summer internship ending soon, I asked the elders of that church if they could recommend a similar type of church for me to attend in Virginia. They suggested I check out a church in Washington, DC—two hours from the UVA campus. I called their office, and they in turn recommended a Maranatha church—now called Grace Covenant Church—in Charlottesville. On the following Saturday morning, I arrived at their doorstep and knocked. When the door opened, I introduced myself: "Hi! My name is Manny Carlos. I'm an international student, and I want to be discipled."

Later I discovered why my introduction was so astounding to them. Maranatha's campus ministries were located on and around university campuses and focused on evangelism and discipleship among college students. At one point, Maranatha embraced the vision for international students. The idea was to win, disciple, and send international students back to their countries to plant churches and campus ministries. It was not only a good idea, it was a vision that was actually working. Their campus ministries had a growing number of internationals attending their meetings and even staff dedicated to that particular outreach. Since Maranatha at UVA did not have international students in their church, it had become an ongoing emphasis at their prayer meetings. When I showed up at their door announcing, "My name is Manny Carlos. I am an international student, and I want to be discipled," the student at the door was dumbfounded. Thinking back on that event reminds me of Peter's miraculous delivery and the servant girl Rhoda in Acts 12.

> *When he realized this, he went to the house of Mary, the mother of John whose other name was Mark, where many were gathered together and were praying. And when he knocked at the door of the gateway, a servant girl named Rhoda came to answer. Recognizing Peter's voice, in her joy she did not open the gate but ran in and reported that Peter was standing at the gate. They said to her, "You are out of your mind...."*
>
> —ACTS 12:12–15

· · ·

The UVA student did answer when I knocked, and they were all likewise astounded. And there it was again—extraordinary guidance by an unseen hand in answer to prayer. The Maranatha church was part of the organization that had sent Pastor Rice, Pastor Steve, and the American team to Manila. It's the kind of momentary glimpse into the unseen hand of God's providence that gives you goosebumps. Looking back now, the sovereignty of God seems inescapable. For those who are called to his purpose, it's harder to miss God's leading than we may think.

Written by John, the book of Revelation is about the last days before the second coming of Christ. It contains a passage about an angel offering incense, along with the prayers of the saints, before the throne of God. It seems that there is an eternal remembrance or record in heaven of every prayer and petition offered as a sacrifice to God (Revelation 8:2–4). At so many critical junctures in my life, the prayers of others have led and even propelled me along the path of God's purpose. And with each turn of events, my appreciation of the importance of prayer continued to increase. After all, I was certain that through the prayers of my mother, my eyes had been opened, my resistant heart softened, and my faith emboldened. Mom continued to pray for her family, and within the next decade, each of my three siblings was born again. When she passed away in 2017 after a lingering illness, we knew she would receive a rich welcome into God's kingdom for her faith in Christ, her dedication to prayer, and her witness to us all.

In retrospect, the sovereignty of God often seems inescapable.

Lord, I thank you for pursuing me and redeeming my life. How awesome is your mercy and grace toward me! Forgive me for my forgetfulness of your providence ever working in my life. I lay all my disappointments at your feet and trust that in time all things will have worked together for the good of those who love you and are called according to your purpose (Romans 8:28).

The prayers of others propel a person along the path of God's purpose.

Having been pursued by the love of God and the prayers of others, I intercede for <insert friend or family member's name>. Whisper into their ears about your plan and purpose for their lives. I pray that your Holy Spirit would pursue them relentlessly and give them no rest until they each surrender to love, mercy, and forgiveness.

CHAPTER TWO

BIG ON FORM, LOW ON POWER

Are you so foolish? Having begun by the Spirit, are you now being perfected by the flesh?

—GALATIANS 3:3

In one of the first meetings I attended at the UVA Maranatha church, the founding leader of the church movement, Bob Weiner, was the guest speaker. No matter where his messages began, they always ended up challenging students to make a total commitment to Jesus Christ as Lord. Given my rejuvenated faith, Bob's messages particularly resonated with me. I didn't want to be lukewarm, and I didn't want the fire in me to grow cold. I wanted to be a totally committed, sold-out disciple of Jesus.

Not long after I began attending Maranatha, we watched a video series by Pastor Larry Lea based on his book, *Could You Not Tarry One Hour?: Learning the Joy of Prayer.*[1] The title comes from Jesus at the Garden of Gethsemane (Matthew 26:40–41) where Peter, James, and John kept falling asleep while Jesus agonized in prayer over his impending crucifixion. The objective of the video series, also from that passage, was to spend one hour in prayer each day. The book and the video used the Lord's Prayer (Luke 11:1–4) as a guide, prescribing a number of minutes to each part of the passage as well as a suggested list of requests to cover in each of those segments. Complete all the segments and you've "tarried" with the Lord for about an hour.

All of us were excited to pray. Larry Lea did say that a daily prayer regimen starts with desire, then becomes a discipline, and eventually turns into a delight. I thought about that later, but it wasn't my initial focus. The desire was present at the beginning but never progressed to a discipline, let alone a delight. Sustaining the consistency was something I was unable to do. It was frustrating because the video suggested that if we devoted an hour each day to pray through the formula, we would move into a higher realm of the supernatural.

There is a paradox among those wanting to be "totally committed," specifically among Christians whose faith is built on a less-than-solid or even shaky foundation. The paradox is that the more committed you strive to be, the more legalistic you tend to become. That wasn't any of our leaders' intentions. The messages I heard in my early weeks in the church were spot-on for a group of college students. Thankfully, efforts by the church leaders to disciple their on-fire international student helped me eventually understand total commitment in the context of the grace of God and the finished work of Jesus Christ on the cross. It's a life-changing biblical principle—not that hard to understand but not that easy to live out.

Formalism and Legalism

Though I heard later on that some of the churches did indeed have some of those legalistic tendencies, that was not my experience in our church. Pastors Mark Beliles, Robert Baxter, and Taylor Stewart could not have been better examples of greater faith and greater commitment, as well as greater grace.

Legalism, as the apostle Paul defined it, was strict adherence to the Law of Moses as the way to be right with God. In contrast, the gospel of the New Covenant is that the righteousness of God is reckoned or imputed, not on the basis for the Old Testament Law but to those who believe. There is a parallel between Jews who trust in the Law of Moses and Gentiles who trust in their knowledge or good behavior for their salvation. I think the pitfall that others and I wandered into was more formalism than legalism. In other words, we got excited about replicating a form or methodology of prayer with the sincere hope that the form itself would empower our prayer life. Formalism is putting your hope in a form without the power of the Holy Spirit.

In the previous church I attended in White Plains, New York, I learned about *The 2959 Plan: A Guide to Communion with God*, written and taught by the great pastor-teacher, Peter Lord. This was another formula for prayer that was to motivate believers to pray for half an hour, or twenty-nine minutes and fifty-nine seconds each day. At UVA we got excited about Larry Lea's *Could You Not Tarry One Hour?* system of prayer based on the story of Jesus in Matthew 26:40–41. A few months later, someone commented on the story from Luke 6:12. Referring to Jesus, it says, "In these days he went out to the mountain to pray, and all night he continued in prayer to God." Surely, following the Lord's example in praying all night would have profound significance. That was the beginning of the Maranatha Satellite Prayer Network. Once a month, churches across the nation would tune in at midnight for a prayer meeting that lasted till 6:00 a.m. or whatever time it was in their city. I remember there was a lot of praying as leaders would take turns standing in front of the camera to pray. It was, to say the least, pretty intense.

The difference between the pitfalls of formalism and legalism is that when you fail to live up to formalistic standards, you feel disappointed because the form or system didn't produce the abundant life you had hoped it would. If you fail to live up to legalistic standards, the result is condemnation. It would be as if Jesus prodded you to pray and then demanded that you explain why you could not tarry with him for one hour.

Did all of those systems of prayer bear fruit? Yes, absolutely. I believe many who were saved, discipled, and sent into all the world to preach the gospel, including those who planted Victory in Metro Manila, were the result of those prayers. Nevertheless, there is something superficial about looking to a form or system of prayer as the source of spiritual empowerment. That is as true with charismatic forms as it is for centuries-old liturgies. The longer you follow a legalistic or formalistic path to prayer, the less meaningful it becomes. It can feel like driving down a muddy road and your tires start to spin. The more you step on the gas pedal, the more the car gets stuck and sinks into the mud.

In one of his messages, Dr. Darren Whitehead outlined the progression of those trying to pursue God's purposes for them in the power of the flesh rather than in the power of the Holy Spirit. We can probably relate with some of the legalistic or formalistic responses he identified.

Our first response is to try harder. We'll get up earlier because we heard other people get up early to pray. That lasts for a little while, but we can't sustain it. Eventually, we feel discouraged and a little bit disillusioned.

Secondly, we begin to pretend that we're more spiritual than we are. We talk about our prayer time or even about God speaking to us. Each time, however, we experience a tinge of conviction because we know that we're just faking it—and God knows too.

The third response when people are not experiencing the victory or abundant life that had been promised to them is that they rededicate their lives. Some are on a continuous cycle of determination, discouragement, quitting, and rededication.

Our fourth response is to change churches. "The teaching is not deep enough, the music is not the right style, the pastor spends too much time on the offering. It's not working for me here anymore." And when none of these things work, people just eventually give up. They remain Christians and church attenders, but inwardly, they've decided that it's not possible to overcome the debilitating power of the flesh.[2]

Easy Does It

My Catholic upbringing instilled in me the need to pray, not that I prayed very much. I just lived with a sense of obligation while at the same time a spiritual uncertainty hung over me. What it did not teach me was how to have a prayer life flowing from communion with God. The few times I did pray, the practice seemed rote and routine. I was taught to recite certain prayers, but I didn't have the vocabulary to express my heart to God.

Praying is not that difficult. With a little effort and humility, anyone can do it. Communion with God that empowers consistent spiritual disciplines—that's another matter. It does require more time and less distraction, more focus and less formality. But it's **not** about more effort. In the early days when I led prayer meetings in our church, I would observe how several of our intercessors seemed to have a greater boldness to approach God and articulate their prayers with confidence, yet with respect, like a son or daughter wanting something from a father or mother.

Christians who focus primarily on requests rather than communion can at times seem to be talking to someone with whom they have a distant or even uncertain relationship. After running through a laundry list of needs, they think to themselves, *Okay, what do I say now?* They stumble through the conversation, desperately trying to avoid those awkward moments of silence. In broadcasting, they call this "dead air." Consequently, the language of prayer becomes redundant, repetitive, and quite unnatural. If those conversations with God were transcribed, what an odd and mechanical relationship it would suggest! Having said all that's on their mind, they begin to get anxious and decide it's time to get on to other business.

This is not so unlike Jesus' parable of the prodigal son (Luke 15:11–32). It was not told as something that actually happened but as an illustration used to create a teaching moment. It could have easily been based on a real event in the life of Jesus or his community. After all, stories of greedy heirs and broken relationships with the accumulators of wealth have been told and retold, lived and relived since the beginning of time. In most of those stories, whether fact or fiction, heirs circle like vultures, waiting impatiently, even wishing that the old guy would hurry up and die. The younger son in Jesus' story was anxious to be enriched by his father's inheritance, so much so that he thought about it constantly—how his life would change when he became a rich young man. Of course, the young man pretended to love his father because revealing his true feelings could cost him dearly when the inheritance was finally dispersed. Remember, he was the younger brother, and the lion's share traditionally went to the oldest son.

The teaching point of the parable highlighted the father's unconditional love and forgiveness—that this is what our Father in heaven is like. However, it also reveals something about the focus and motivation of our prayer lives. Our heavenly Father loves us and wants to bless us, but what he desires more than anything is to have a deep, loving relationship—for us to love spending time with him and for communion and fellowship to be the priority of our relationship. If our prayer life is dominated by our needs and wants apart from our need and want of his presence, then it is like a father with children who long for the stuff he can give far more than they long for him.

· · ·

Jesus asked, "So, could you not watch with me one hour?" In the next verse, he said, "The spirit indeed is willing, but the flesh is weak" (Matthew 26:41). People typically zero in on the last part of the sentence—"but the flesh is weak." Oh yes, we all know that the flesh is weak. But more importantly, Jesus said, "The spirit is willing . . ."

Really?

So, the Holy Spirit empowers our prayer lives if we are willing, despite our fleshly weakness? Maybe Pastor Lea was right but just had it backwards. When assuring listeners that one hour of prayer each day would elevate them into a realm of the supernatural, it was actually the realm of the supernatural that would empower a meaningful prayer life. The empowerment to pray and the power of prayer is in the presence of the Spirit, not the discipline or determination of the flesh.

A consistent, passionate, and effective prayer life doesn't originate with a sense of need, even the needs of others. Neither is it simply presenting your list of requests to God. Many who are unaccustomed to this priority and approach (those in the habit of storming heaven with needs, requests, and wants) have difficulty and are uncomfortable sitting quietly in God's presence. A life of prayer flows from ongoing fellowship with the Spirit and the invitation to partner with the Father in seeing his kingdom come on earth as it is in heaven. If we do not seek first and desire God's presence and God's pleasure, then we come to his table not as heirs to the promise but like beggars waiting for the next crumb to fall.

A consistent, passionate, and effective prayer life doesn't originate with a sense of need, even the needs of others, but from ongoing communion with God.

Tune my heart, oh Lord, to be sensitive to your Spirit calling me to spend time in your presence. Forgive me for turning away and resisting your invitation, for the want of other things to occupy my thoughts and activities.

The flesh is weak, but the Holy Spirit is willing to empower my prayer life.

Lord, fill me and empower me with the unction to intercede on behalf of your kingdom purposes. May the passion of Jesus flow through me to stand in the gap for those in need, and let me feel the force of your love for those you have called to yourself.

Replicating a form or methodology of prayer will not automatically produce a Spirit-empowered prayer life.

Without your presence, I am unable to do the things I know that I should do. The desire is in me, but the power is not. Forgive me for thinking I could do your will by my own strength or by my own resolve. I am dependent upon you for my steadfastness, for my spiritual disciplines, for my sanctification. Apart from you, there is no limit to how far I might fall.

If my prayer life is dominated by my needs and wants apart from my need and want of God's presence, I am like a spoiled child who longs for stuff far more than longing for the Father.

Forgive me for seeking your blessings far more than I desire your presence.

CHAPTER THREE

RADICAL SIMPLICITY

I am afraid that, as the serpent deceived Eve by his craftiness, your minds will be led astray from the simplicity and purity of devotion to Christ.

—2 CORINTHIANS 11:3-4 (NASB)

How did the ministry and message of Jesus Christ evolve over the centuries into such liturgical forms of prayer and complex formulas for spiritual growth? And how did some expressions of Protestantism become so theologically mechanical and resistant to the moving of the Holy Spirit? It is quite difficult to connect the dots between the very early church and its modern-day expressions. As disciples striving to walk in the Spirit and be empowered by an ongoing communion with God, my concern is similar to the apostle Paul's concern for members of the church in Corinth—that their "minds be led astray from the simplicity and purity of devotion to Christ" (2 Corinthians 11:3-4, NASB)—the keywords being **simplicity** and **devotion**.

I've tried to imagine what it was like for the twelve disciples who were the primary followers of Jesus. Rabbis traditionally imposed strict rules of discipline upon their disciples, a practice that Jesus vehemently opposed: "Woe to you, scribes and Pharisees, hypocrites! For you travel across sea and land to make a single proselyte, and when he becomes a proselyte, you make him twice as much a child of hell as yourselves" (Matthew 23:15). That's one of the hardest sayings of Jesus. That kind of condemnation would not apply to those Jesus would send into the world to make disciples of all nations (Matthew 28:18–20; Mark 16:15–16). He pronounced the woes upon the disciple-making practices of the scribes and Pharisees because of their twisted and self-righteous motivations—legalism, formalism, and hypocrisy. In stark contrast, the disciples of Jesus had quite a different experience. It was never about adopting the disciplines of Jesus, the Teacher (Rabbi), but all about personal devotion and a love relationship with him. In fact, the only evidence for the institution of a formal regimen of spiritual disciplines among the Twelve was the lack thereof. That was evident to others, particularly to the disciples of John the Baptist. They questioned Jesus about why he had not created more rules and practices for spiritual growth.

> *Then the disciples of John came to him, saying, "Why do we and the Pharisees fast, but your disciples do not fast?" And Jesus said to them, "Can the wedding guests mourn as long as the bridegroom is with them? The days will come when the bridegroom is taken away from them, and then they will fast."*
> — MATTHEW 9:14–15

The obvious absence of rules in the tradition of John the Baptist among Jesus and the Twelve persisted. Finally, one of the disciples (perhaps speaking the concerns of others) asked Jesus for more specifics on how they should pray. Apparently, the Rabbi Jesus had given no formula or method of prayer; he just prayed.

> *Now Jesus was praying in a certain place, and when he finished, one of his disciples said to him, "Lord, teach us to pray, as John taught his disciples."*
> — LUKE 11:1

What followed has come to be known as the Lord's Prayer. I don't think Jesus intended for that response to become the standardized liturgical prayer that it has. If so, he probably would have given those prescribed words long before. As it was, Jesus answered the question, perhaps because they had failed to learn from his example. Or perhaps that particular disciple was uncomfortable with the absence of rules and was just looking for a more formalized rule of discipline. Jesus seemed to be asking:

So, you actually need a formula for talking to your Father? Okay, if you have to have a formal prayer, pray like this.

Following Jesus was a roller coaster ride—very unpredictable, informal, and relational. Jesus was constantly bending or breaking the rules and doing the unexpected, following the will of the Father and the leading of the Spirit. It was everything pharisaical discipleship was not. Spiritual formation is not accomplished by a program, class, or formula. As Pastor Joey Bonifacio, a dear friend and fellow pastor in Every Nation, has said repeatedly, "Discipleship is relationship"—relationship with God and with one another.

Since Jesus seemed to be reluctant to impose a formula for prayer or spiritual formation upon his disciples, why should I add to that simplicity? In response to a Pharisee's question about the greatest commandment, Jesus said:

"You shall love the Lord your God with all your heart and with all your soul and with all your mind. This is the great and first commandment. And a second is like it: You shall love your neighbor as yourself."

—MATTHEW 22:37-39

This Pharisee was perhaps looking for a formula by which to justify himself before God. Pharisees were so addicted to that way of thinking that only a few could rise above it. However, Jesus gave a radically simplified answer and concluded with the comment: "On these two commandments depend all the Law and the Prophets" (Matthew 22:40). Since it seemed to Jesus that it was enough to demonstrate how to pray rather than prescribe systematic forms of prayer, I thought it best to include a brief summary of one whose method of prayer and communion with God was equally simple.

Lawrence of the Resurrection

There is no one I have ever known or read about who was more dedicated to Christ and more successful in cultivating the presence of God than Nicholas Herman. He was born in 1614 in the region bordering Germany and France, was taught the fear of God by his parents, and, as a young man, was drafted into the army as a French soldier in the Thirty Years' War. He left the army after being severely wounded, spent a few years as a religious hermit, and at the age of twenty-six became a novitiate among the Discalced Carmelite monks. He adopted the name Lawrence of the Resurrection, more commonly known simply as Brother Lawrence.

The order was named "Carmelite" in honor of a small band of twelfth-century European Christians who had gathered in Palestine near Mount Carmel, most famously known as the site where Elijah challenged the prophets of Baal and called fire down from heaven. It was there that this group of Christians dedicated themselves to live as hermits on the mountain and spend their lives in contemplation of Christ's crucifixion and resurrection. The Discalced Carmelites were established by St. Teresa of Avila in 1562 and St. John of the Cross in 1568 to renew the order's commitment to contemplation, simplicity, and community.

The Discalced Carmelite Order was a more radically ascetic offshoot of the Carmelites. The word "discalced" meant without shoes. Their objective was strict adherence to the Rule of Saint Albert, which involved a lot more than going barefooted. Besides the general rules of celibacy, poverty, and strict obedience, the Rule of Saint Albert, like many of the monastic orders, contained a dizzying number of rules and regulations regarding every waking moment of the day—far too many for the purpose of this chapter. Concerning the form and discipline of daily prayer, the Primitive Rule stipulated the following:

Those who do not know the hours must say twenty-five "Our Father" for the night office, except on Sundays and solemnities when that number is to be doubled so that the "Our Father" is said fifty times; the same prayer must be said seven times in the morning in place of Lauds, and seven times too for each of the other hours, except for Vespers when it must be said fifteen times.[1]

—THE PRIMITIVE RULE OF THE ORDER OF THE BLESSED VIRGIN MARY OF MOUNT CARMEL

The Carmelite Order still exists today and attracts many followers seeking a deeper and more meaningful experience with God. The previous paragraphs are not meant to be a commentary on the modern-day Carmelite Brothers, but only as an introduction to their most notable Brother Lawrence. All monastic orders have detailed recommendations (if not strict regulations) on spiritual disciplines, the purposes of which are to create an ongoing communion with God. For the Corinthian believers to whom the apostle Paul wrote and the Carmelite Brothers (from the middle ages to the present), it's not that I question their devotion, but that the departure from simplicity seems to load believers down with a very heavy burden. The primary thing they both had in common with Pharisees of the first century is that the average Israelite didn't have time for the complex set of rules and regulations. One had to be a full-time religious professional to follow all the rules.

My first exposure to the story and the rule of discipline of Brother Lawrence was in 1988 in a little sixty-page booklet entitled *The Practice of the Presence of God*. All that is known about him comes from a collection of four conversations and a dozen short letters. Ironically, the conversations were private, and he only agreed to write the letters upon the condition that they would never be seen by anyone else. Without such an agreement, he refused to call attention to himself by corresponding with the outside world.

Brother Lawrence was much like Maria von Trapp, whose life was portrayed in the 1959 Broadway musical and the 1965 Academy Award-winning Best Picture, *The Sound of Music*. In a 1980 speech at the Catholic Family Life Conference, the seventy-five-year-old matriarch recalled that she decided to join the Benedictine Abbey of Nonnberg in Salzburg as a novice because it was the strictest convent she could find. Maria von Trapp told the crowd, "I was horrid, the worst you can imagine." According to her speech and books, she broke china, spoke during periods of silence, ran through the courtyard, slid down banisters, whistled Gregorian chants, and climbed on the convent roof.[2] "Those two years were really necessary to get my twisted character and my overgrown self-will cut down to size."[3] Maria was not very good at conforming to the rigid spiritual disciplines of the Benedictine Order. Consequently, I couldn't but be reminded of her when I first read about Brother Lawrence.

The title, *The Practice of the Presence of God,* sounds like a how-to book—a step-by-step recipe guaranteed to summon up God's presence and power. But nothing could be farther from the truth. From the time he joined the Discalced Carmelite Order, Brother Lawrence had a burning passion to know God and to live in his presence. However, it took him about a decade to work through his frustrations as well as his bouts with condemnation. Eventually, his passionate love for God and desire to live each moment in his presence led to a radically simplified approach to spiritual disciplines.

The Abbé Joseph de Beaufort recorded his four conversations with Brother Lawrence, who, when pressed to explain himself, responded out of obligation to his superior. Father Beaufort also collected the twelve letters Brother Lawrence wrote to Reverend Mother N. Reading through a few of Brother Lawrence's thoughts on the method of spiritual formation that he followed for thirty years, you'll see why it is so inspiring to me. These are my top ten takeaways from the comments of Brother Lawrence along with my own prayers of consecration.[4]

Brother Lawrence's rule of discipline was radically simple.

His single act of spiritual discipline (beyond what was required of him) was to think about God as often as he could, and he accustomed himself by degrees to this small but holy exercise. When outward business diverted him a little from the thought of God, a fresh remembrance coming from God invested his soul and so inflamed and transported him that it was difficult for him to contain himself.

"A little lifting up of the heart suffices," he said. "A little remembrance of God, one act of inward worship . . . however short, are nevertheless very acceptable to God. . . . By frequently renewed acts of faith and love, I am come to a state wherein it would be as difficult for me not to think of God as it was at first to accustom myself to do it."

> **PRAYER FOR SIMPLICITY**
>
> *Forgive me, Lord, for going hours without acknowledging your presence with my praise and worship; for the times I dishonor you by failing to remember your goodness and mercy; for entertaining myself with unbridled thoughts that quench and grieve the Holy Spirit. Lord, constrain my heart to sing your praise, to meditate upon your word, and to think of you as often as I can.*

Brother Lawrence's designated times of prayer did not differ from other times.

Because he developed the habit of thinking about God and worshiping him continually, Brother Lawrence found that he was more unified to God in his outward employments than when he left them for designated times of prayer. His greatest attention to work in the kitchen did not divert him from God or the sense of his presence.

When he began his business in the kitchen, he would pray, "O my God, since thou art with me and I must now, in obedience to thy commands, apply my mind to these outward things, I beseech thee to grant me the grace to continue in thy presence; and to this end do thou prosper me with thy assistance, receive all my works, and possess all my affections."

He also said: "The time of business does not with me differ from the time of prayer; and in the noise and clatter of my kitchen, while several persons are at the same time calling for different things, I possess God in as great tranquility as if I were upon my knees at the blessed sacrament."

He was occasionally sent to Burgundy to buy provisions of wine for the society. It was a very unwelcome task for him because he had no instincts for business and was lame and could not go about the boat but by rolling himself over the casks. However, that and the purchase of the wine gave him no uneasiness. He said to God that he was going about God's business.

PRAYER BEFORE WORK

O my God, since I know that you are with me and that I must now apply my mind to these outward things, grant me the grace to continue in your presence uninterrupted by unholy thoughts. Enable me to conduct my business with the clear awareness that you are watching and weighing my every word, thought, and action. Prosper me with your assistance, receive all my works, and possess all my affections.

We stand before God with great fear and reverence, but speak to him intimately and casually.

Brother Lawrence said: "We ought to act with God in the greatest simplicity, speaking to him frankly and plainly, and imploring his assistance in our affairs, just as they happen. . . . After a little care, we should find his love inwardly excite us to it (talking with him continually) without any difficulty."

PRAYER FOR INTIMATE COMMUNION

Draw me closer that I would have the boldness of Moses who spoke with you face to face, as a man speaks to his friend (Exodus 33:11). And that I would be even more confident to receive the fullness of the Spirit of your Son into my heart, by (and through) whom I cry "Abba! Father!" (Romans 8:15).

Brother Lawrence did not put his trust in the multitude of words nor set forms of prayer.

Brother Lawrence said: "I have quitted all forms of devotion and set prayers but those to which my state obliges me. And I make it my business only to persevere in his holy presence, wherein I keep myself by a simple attention . . . an habitual, silent, and secret conversation of the soul with God, which often causes me joys and raptures inwardly, and sometimes also outwardly, so great, that I am forced to use means to moderate them and prevent their appearance to others. . . . I do not advise you to use multiplicity of words in prayer: many words and long discourses being often the occasions of wandering. Hold yourself in prayer before God, like a dumb or paralytic beggar at a rich man's gate."

PRAYER OF SILENCE

There is no need of which you are not fully aware, and yet my conversation with you often assumes that you are ignorant of all things. Forgive me for being so shallow in my faith. Forgive me for thinking that you are persuaded by my many words or the volume of my prayer rather than my faith in your word, your love, and your grace shown to us by giving your only begotten Son. Teach me to wait upon you and trust you for the things we ask for, that you may accomplish all things according to your will.

We should do all things for the love of God.

Brother Lawrence said: "That there needed neither art nor science for going to God, but only a heart resolutely determined to apply itself to nothing but him. . . . That we ought not to be weary of doing little things for the love of God, who regards not the greatness of the work, but the love with which it is performed."

He found that the most excellent method of going to God was that of doing our common business without any view of pleasing men, but purely for the love of God.

> ### PRAYER OF SURRENDER TO LOVE
>
> *Give me grace to see and to repent of all things that are not done out of love for you and others. Purge out of me the unrelenting bent toward the love of self that refuses to be inconvenienced or closes my ears to your calling for sacrifice. Sanctify me in the most secret and undisclosed closets of my heart that it may be ruled and controlled by divine love.*

Brother Lawrence's love for God was unconditional.

"I engaged in a religious life only for the love of God," he told Father Beaufort, "and I have endeavored to act only for **h**im; whatever becomes of me, whether I be lost or saved, I will always continue to act purely for the love of God. I shall have this good at least, that until death I shall have done all that is in me to love **h**im." That, of course, reminds us of the word of the apostle Paul who wrote, ". . . I could wish that I myself were accursed and cut off from Christ for the sake of my brothers, my kinsmen according to the flesh" (Romans 9:3).

> ### PRAYER FOR CONTENTMENT
>
> *I pray that Christ may dwell in my heart through faith—that being rooted and grounded in love, I may be able to comprehend with*

all the saints what is the breadth and length and height and depth, and to know the love of Christ that surpasses knowledge, that I might be filled with all the fullness of God (Ephesians 3:17–19).

Brother Lawrence adopted a "rule of discipline" and pursued it faithfully for twenty-six years without the slightest tinge of condemnation.

Initially, Brother Lawrence battled with condemnation from his wandering mind and constant failure in his duties. He was lame from a war injury, notoriously awkward, and worked in the kitchen of the monastery for over thirty years. For the first four years, he labored under the certain belief that he would be damned, and all the men in the world could not persuade him to the contrary. Somewhere along the way, whether from Scripture or from assurances from his time with God, his confessions of faith became as theologically reformed as those of John Calvin or Martin Luther. His righteousness-consciousness seemed even more secure and founded in grace through faith in the finished work of Jesus Christ.

"That this trouble of mind had lasted four years: during which time he had suffered much. But that at last, he had seen that this trouble arose from want of faith; and that since then he had passed his life in perfect liberty and continual joy." Though he was very sensible of his faults, Brother Lawrence was neither discouraged nor condemned. He confessed them to God and continued his practice of love and adoration. "That, without being discouraged on account of our sins, we should pray for his grace with a perfect confidence, as relying upon the infinite merits of our Lord Jesus Christ."

PRAYER OF FAITH

Lord, after all is said and done, I am a sinner and an unfaithful servant. On my own merits, I would be eternally lost, without God and without the least hope of redemption. Nevertheless, I lay the whole weight of my trust in the sacrifice of your Son, Jesus, and I receive by faith the gift of righteousness.

If our minds wander during the time of prayer, God welcomes our return without condemnation.

In the beginning, Brother Lawrence had often passed his time appointed for prayer in rejecting wandering thoughts and subsequently falling back into them. He could never regulate his devotion by certain methods as some do. At first, he had meditated for some time but, afterward, he wandered off in a manner for which he could give no account.

Brother Lawrence said: "Having found in many books different methods of going to God, and diverse practices of the spiritual life, I thought this would serve rather to puzzle me than facilitate what I sought after . . . I worshiped him the oftenest that I could, keeping my mind in his holy presence, and recalling it as often as I found it wandered from him . . . without troubling or disquieting myself when my mind had wandered involuntarily. . . . For at all times, every hour, every minute, even in the height of my business, I drove away from my mind everything that was capable of interrupting my thought of God. . . . I do not say that therefore we must put any violent constraint upon ourselves. No, we must serve God in a holy freedom; we must do our business faithfully; without trouble or disquiet, recalling our mind to God mildly, and with tranquility, as often as we find it wandering from him."

PRAYER FOR WANDERING MINDS

Forgive me for my wandering thoughts; for my lack of attention to the God whose eye is always upon me; and for my passionless prayers to the God whose passion for me was demonstrated on the cross. Though my failures in prayer seem never-ending, I will return to you again and again because of the great love with which you have loved me.

Brother Lawrence did not let his failures or infirmities separate him from the sense of God's presence.

He was very sensible of his faults but not discouraged by them. He confessed them to God saying, "I shall never do otherwise, if you leave me to myself; it is you who must hinder my falling, and mend what is amiss. That after this, he gave himself no further uneasiness about it."

PRAYER TO SURRENDER OUR FAILURES

I lay all the gifts and talents you have bestowed upon me before you. Do with them and with me as you please. Forgive me of pride in my abilities, for I could have accomplished nothing without your assistance. Take my abilities and sanctify them for your use. I give you my weaknesses and faults. I could never do this without the power of the Holy Spirit.

Brother Lawrence did not consider his simple approach to prayer a hard thing to accomplish.

Having accustomed himself to doing everything for the love of God and with prayer for his grace, he found everything to be done with ease. "Were I a preacher," he said, "I should, above all other things, preach the practice of the presence of God; and, were I a director, I should advise all the world to do it, so necessary do I think it, and so easy, too."

PRAYER OF DEDICATION

Lord Jesus, I devote myself to prayer as the earliest disciples did, knowing that my only hope of overcoming my fleshly temptations and of changing my lifestyle is the empowering presence of the Holy Spirit. Fill me with your Spirit again and again and again.

A rule of discipline can be radically simple.

Forgive me, Lord, for going hours without acknowledging your presence with my praise and worship; for the times I dishonor you by failing to remember your goodness and mercy; for entertaining myself with unbridled thoughts that quench and grieve the Holy Spirit. Lord, constrain my heart to sing your praise, to meditate upon your word, and to think of you as often as I can.

Designated times of prayer need not differ from other times.

O my God, since I know that you are with me and that I must now apply my mind to these outward things, grant me the grace to continue in your presence uninterrupted by unholy thoughts. Enable me to conduct my business with the clear awareness that you are watching and weighing my every word, thought, and action. Prosper me with your assistance, receive all my works, and possess all my affections.

We should stand before God with great fear and reverence but speak to him intimately and casually.

Draw me closer that I would have the boldness of Moses who spoke with you face to face, as a man speaks to his friend (Exodus 33:11). And that I would be even more confident to receive the fullness of the Spirit of your Son into my heart, by (and through) whom I cry "Abba! Father!" (Romans 8:15).

Do not put your trust in the multitude of words nor in set forms of prayer.

There is no need of which you are not fully aware, and yet my conversation with you often assumes that you are ignorant of all things. Forgive me for being so shallow in my faith. Forgive me for thinking that you are persuaded by my many words or the volume of my prayer rather than my faith in your word, your love, and your grace shown to us by giving your only begotten Son. Teach me to wait upon you and trust you for the things we ask for, that you may accomplish all things according to your will.

We should do all things for the love of God.

Give me grace to see and to repent of all things that are not done out of love for you and others. Purge out of me the unrelenting bent toward the love of self that refuses to be inconvenienced or closes my ears to your calling for sacrifice. Sanctify me in the most secret and undisclosed closets of my heart that it may be ruled and controlled by divine love.

We should love God unconditionally.

I pray that Christ may dwell in my heart through faith—that being rooted and grounded in love, I may be able to comprehend with all the saints what is the breadth and length and height and depth, and to know the love of Christ that surpasses knowledge, that I might be filled with all the fullness of God (Ephesians 3:17–19).

Adopt a "rule of discipline" and pursue it faithfully without condemnation.

Lord, after all is said and done, I am a sinner and an unfaithful servant. On my own merits, I would be eternally lost, without God and without the least hope of redemption. Nevertheless, I lay the whole weight of my trust in the sacrifice of your Son, Jesus, and I receive by faith the gift of righteousness.

If our minds wander during the time of prayer, God welcomes our return without condemnation.

Forgive me for my wandering thoughts; for my lack of attention to the God whose eye is always upon me; and for my passionless prayers to the God whose passion for me was demonstrated on the cross. Though my failures in prayer seem never-ending, I will return to you again and again because of the great love with which you have loved me.

Do not let failures or infirmities separate you from the sense of God's presence.

I lay all the gifts and talents you have bestowed upon me before you. Do with them and with me as you please. Forgive me of pride in my abilities, for I could have accomplished nothing without your assistance. Take my abilities and sanctify them for your use. I give you my weaknesses and faults. I could never do this without the power of the Holy Spirit.

A simple approach to prayer is not a hard thing to accomplish.

Lord Jesus, I devote myself to prayer as the earliest disciples did, knowing that my only hope of overcoming my fleshly temptations and of changing my lifestyle is the empowering presence of the Holy Spirit. Fill me with your Spirit again and again and again.

CHAPTER FOUR

HONORING THE PRESENCE

Discipline yourself for the purpose of godliness.
—1 TIMOTHY 4:7 (NASB)

Programmed spiritual disciplines are less relevant or even irrelevant to those whose hearts and minds are already filled with a passionate love for God and burning desire to please him. Father Beaufort commented on the motivation and the outcome of Brother Lawrence's radically simplified approach: "... having accustomed himself to do everything for the love of God ... he found everything easy." For a believer who is unconditionally surrendered, established in the righteousness of Christ, and empowered by the Holy Spirit, there is no striving in spiritual disciplines. The believer simply lets it happen.

In the previous chapters, I have been making the case for a kind of anti-formalism—that is, walking in the Spirit rather than trying to follow a rigid spiritual discipline. Jesus and the apostle Paul made the case against our tendency to rely on a form or regimen of prayer as the source of abundant life. Genuine communion with God through the Holy Spirit is rarely formal or mechanical. Jesus said about the Holy Spirit's inspiration in prayer: "You have received the Spirit of adoption as sons, **by whom** we cry, 'Abba! Father!'" (Romans 8:15). When the Holy Spirit inspires and empowers one's prayer life, it often becomes shockingly informal and unashamedly bold (Luke 11:8). That assumed relationship was so radically different from traditional forms of prayer, the first-century religious leaders cried, "Blasphemy!" while the Holy Spirit wanted to cry out, "Abba! Father!" This is evidence of the astounding outpouring of God's grace—the transcendent glory, power, and unapproachable holiness of Almighty God juxtaposed to the grace of God in Jesus Christ by which we talk with him in the language of a child with his daddy.

Not every Christian is "so longing" for that kind of close communion with God as was the all-consuming desire of Brother Lawrence and countless other passionate followers throughout church history. The cost of unconditional surrender is quite high, and the comfort of our lives is often very great. Many choose to follow Christ, but like Peter on the night of Christ's betrayal, many of those choose to "follow at a distance" (Mark 14:54). Despite his bold promise to be faithful unto death, we know what happened to Peter on the night of Christ's arrest. By the time the rooster crowed, Peter had denied Jesus three times.

Spiritual transformation, otherwise known as sanctification, is not the result of human striving or spiritual exercises but of the power of the Holy Spirit to transform us into Christ's image with Christ's character, Christ's perspective, and Christ's priorities. This is what it means to be a disciple of Christ—one who follows him not at a distance but fully and passionately. For those who have cultivated the habit of spending time in his presence, it is not considered a cost at all but the greatest privilege.

Lest you think that I consider myself to be the follower who is already totally committed and totally surrendered, let me disabuse you of that notion straightaway. There are many untested and unproven areas in my own life, to be sure—challenges to my faith, my surrender without condition, and my love for God above all else. That is to say, I am a follower of Jesus but only as closely as I am following him at this very moment. Discipleship is not a club to join, a doctrinal confession, or a theological position. It is a journey and a growing relationship with God through the empowering presence of the Holy Spirit.

• • •

The idea that our initial experience of being born of the Spirit will be so transforming that it will propel us indefinitely to prayer, surrender, generous giving, serving, and sacrificing as we ought is a very idealistic notion that almost never happens. Rarely is our initial spiritual experience so great that we can simply coast the rest of the way through our Christian life. That's like people in desperate situations who promise to serve God faithfully for the rest of their lives "if only he would . . ." Their desperation is very real, but their determination without his empowering presence is woefully lacking. The pitfall for those who have not felt that kind of love or passion for a long time (or maybe have never felt a sense of God's love) is trying to conjure up some kind of dramatic spiritual experience. Others may resort to methods and schemes that advertise the promise of a deeper communion with God. As I've already said, people eventually grow weary and discouraged that the formulas they followed with great expectations did not produce the abundant life that they had hoped it would.

An unconsecrated heart (no matter what method of prayer you employ) will always be at enmity with God—engaged in a constant battle of his will versus ours. The only prospect for peace is to eventually surrender to one or the other—to the flesh and the works it produces or to the Holy Spirit and the fruit that grows out of that relationship. "No one can serve two masters. Either you will hate the one and love the other, or you will be devoted to the one and despise the other" (Matthew 6:24). Spiritual disciplines are more of an act of submission than assault. Instead of attacking our many enemies, which are our fleshly desires, we should focus on continual surrender to God's person and presence.

The Fruit of Communion

On the one hand, bearing genuine fruit of the Spirit is a miraculous process, or better yet, the result of God's empowering and transforming presence. On the other hand, sowing and cultivating in the Spirit is a discipline (Galatians 6:8). We should be careful not to get the two mixed up. All too often, we put the cart before the horse when it comes to spiritual disciplines. We try to manufacture the fruit of the Holy Spirit by a method or by the force of our will when what we should be doing is planting and cultivating the seeds in our hearts that will naturally (in time) bear fruit of the Spirit thirty-, sixty-, and a hundred-fold.

Richard J. Foster, author of the devotional classic *Celebration of Discipline,* commented on the relationship between the intentional discipline of simplicity (what we supply) and the empowering grace of the Holy Spirit (what he supplies):

> A pivotal paradox for us to understand is that simplicity is both a grace and a discipline . . . Simplicity is a grace because it is given to us by God. There is no way we can build up our willpower or put ourselves into this or that contortion to attain it. It is a gift to be graciously received . . . Simplicity is also a discipline because it calls us to do something . . . What we do does not give us simplicity, but it does put us in the place where we can receive it. It sets our lives before God in such a way that he can work into us the grace of simplicity . . . Perhaps we should learn to speak of "disciplined grace."[1]

Those spiritual disciplines or "holy habits" (as Richard Foster calls them) put us in a frame of mind and heart to be filled and empowered with the Holy Spirit, and it's not a one-time event. The book of Acts refers to repeated fillings with the Spirit (Acts 4:8, 31; 13:9, 52). When the apostle Paul wrote in Ephesians 5:18–19, "Do not get drunk with wine, for that is debauchery, but be filled with the Spirit," he used the present-continuous tense in Greek—that is to say, "be being filled with the Spirit." Whatever the need of the moment—more peace, more power, more joy, more patience, more guidance, more boldness, more awareness of God's presence—being filled with the Holy Spirit is almost always the answer. Consequently, maintaining those holy habits is like planting the seeds that produce the fruit of the Spirit. The author of the book of Hebrews put it quite straightforwardly: "All discipline (even self-discipline) for the moment seems not to be joyful, but sorrowful; yet to those who have been trained by it, afterwards it yields the peaceful fruit of righteousness" (Hebrews 12:11).

J. I. Packer's book *Knowing God* had a profound influence on the way I think about communing with God. I first read it in 1986 during my three-month internship in New York and recently read it again. We don't "know God" by a single experience, but through a lifelong journey (whenever that journey begins) of surrender and time in his presence. Daniel and his covenant brothers are a key example of the fruit of knowing God. They maintained their commitment and their spiritual disciplines at the impending sacrifice of their lives. When they were ordered to eat meat sacrificed to idols, they chose vegetables instead (Daniel 1:12–16). When King Darius passed a law forbidding prayer to anyone but himself, Daniel continued his daily prayer to Jehovah three times a day and was thrown into the lions' den (Daniel 6:6–9). When Nebuchadnezzar ordered everyone to bow before the golden image he had set up, Daniel's three friends were the only ones left standing. When ordered to renounce their crimes of non-compliance, they chose the fiery furnace instead (Daniel 3:1–30). Daniel comments on their combined experiences, "The people that do **know their God** shall be strong, and do exploits" (Daniel 11:32, KJV). That kind of boldness, peace, and resolve is not the fruit of following a legalistic formula. It comes from knowing God through regular communion with him.

The Lord's Vineyard

The Old Testament consistently uses the metaphor of the people of God as the "planting of the Lord" or the "Lord's vineyard" (Psalm 80:14–15; Isaiah 3:13–15; 5:1–3; 5:6–8; Jeremiah 12:10–11). Then in the New Testament parables, Jesus consistently portrayed the Father as the owner of the vineyard. In Matthew 20:1–16, he was the master of a house who hired laborers and sent them out into his vineyard. In Mark 12:1–12, he was the man who planted a vineyard and leased it to tenant farmers who refused to share the produce and finally killed the son who was sent to call them to account. In the parable of the two sons (Matthew 21:28–32), the father sent his two boys out to work in his vineyard. Both refused, but one later decided to obey his father. All of this talk about sowing, reaping, and vineyards that do or don't bear fruit suggests that we should refocus our thinking about communion with God as something that needs to be intentionally cultivated. What, then, are some of the habits or spiritual disciplines we need to continually sow in our lives that will bear the fruit of an ongoing, ever-increasing, and ever-empowering communion with God?

The Habit of Remembering God's Love

Brother Lawrence, whom I have chosen as a primary model, submitted to the disciplines of the Carmelite Brothers, but the rule (or discipline) was certainly not the primary source of his communion with God. In fact, the first four years of the Carmelite Rule of Discipline was almost what did him in spiritually. Though well intended, the Rule of Saint Albert for prayer and spiritual formation was quite a heavy burden. In contrast, the radically simplified spiritual disciplines of Brother Lawrence were, first and foremost, a response to God's love for him and of his love for God. To what extent have we really come to know and comprehend the love of God? In modern secular culture, to say, "God loves you," seems so very trite and common. You might also say that you love food, you love to run, or even that you love your family. Is that all there is to divine love, or is it a woefully inadequate comparison? In Ephesians 3:17–19, the apostle Paul described the goal of our ongoing contemplations this way:

> . . . that you, being rooted and grounded in love, may have strength
> to comprehend with all the saints what is the breadth and length
> and height and depth, and to know the love of Christ that surpasses
> knowledge, that you may be filled with all the fullness of God.

God's love for the saints is with no tinge of hesitation, "no variableness, neither shadow of turning" (James 1:17, KJV). That's what the apostle Paul was hoping the church would understand. It is incomprehensible for an infinitely perfect God to love partially, sparingly, or just a little bit. If God loves us at all, he loves us full-throttle, pedal to the metal, unconditionally, without restraint or restriction. The concept of infinity in the Old Testament is usually described in temporal terminology—"From everlasting to everlasting you are God . . ." (Psalm 90:2) or in spatial terminology, "as high as the heavens are above the earth" (Psalm 103:11). That was the way writers in ancient times described God, who is infinitely perfect in every aspect of the divine nature, including his love. "As high as the heavens are above the earth, so great is his steadfast love toward those who fear him" (Psalm 103:11). In short, his love for us is infinite and absolute, not because we deserve it but only because he has chosen to fix his love upon us. The apostle John wrote: "We have come to know and to believe the love that God has for us. God is love, and whoever abides in love abides in God, and God abides in him" (1 John 4:16). To "abide in that love" and have it abiding in us surpasses any and all efforts to (as Richard Foster put it) "contort ourselves" to attain it.

PERSONAL PRAYER

Oh Lord, open the eyes of my heart that I might behold the breadth and length and height and depth of your great love for me (Ephesians 3:18). May I be consumed by your love, to the end that time in your presence is my insatiable desire.

The Habit of Holy Communion

And he took bread, and when he had given thanks, he broke it and gave it to them, saying, "This is my body, which is given for you. Do this in remembrance of me." And likewise the cup after they had eaten, saying, "This cup that is poured out for you is the new covenant in my blood." (Luke 22:19–20)

When Jesus talked about eating his flesh and drinking his blood (John 6:51), he was speaking metaphorically—just as he was when he said, "'Destroy this temple, and in three days I will raise it up.' . . . But he was speaking about the temple of his body" (John 2:19–21). So, when he said, "This bread is my body and this cup is the new covenant in my blood," he was speaking metaphorically as well. The bread does not supernaturally turn into flesh nor the wine into blood. The main point was remembering, visualizing, and contemplating the redemptive work of Jesus Christ on the cross.

The apostle Paul sheds more light on the practice of eating the bread, drinking wine, and doing it often.

> ". . . Do this in remembrance of me." In the same way also he took the cup, after supper, saying, "This cup is the new covenant in my blood. Do this, as often as you drink it, in remembrance of me." For as often as you eat this bread and drink the cup, you proclaim the Lord's death until he comes.
>
> —1 CORINTHIANS 11:24–26

How often has the church taken something that was intended to occur naturally and organically when believers gathered for worship, and instead institutionalized and formalized it? The point is not about a literal turning of the bread and drink to the body and blood of Christ. Rather, it's about the remembrance of Christ's sacrifice—regularly, daily, or perhaps as often as you have a meal together—that is, as often as you eat and drink. Whether your church celebrates the Lord's Supper monthly, weekly, or every single day—it's not so much about the formality of the ritual. It is about remembering his sacrifice as often as you can.

PERSONAL PRAYER

As I eat this meal and drink from this cup, I remember the sacrifice for my sin and the price you paid for my redemption. And in doing so, I will boldly and joyously proclaim your death and resurrection until your return (1 Corinthians 11:24–26).

The Habit of Remembering Our Desperate Need

The starting point of communion with God is the awareness of what has been accomplished for us by Christ's atoning sacrifice. By grace through faith, we have been "reckoned righteous." That is to say, the righteousness of Christ has been imputed to our account. Consequently, in God's eyes, we stand "blameless before him in the presence of his glory" (Jude 1:24). To put it another way, when we fully apprehend contemplating the depth of our sin and at the same time understand the fullness of what it means to become the righteousness of God in Christ, then and only then can we appreciate the measure of God's grace lavished upon us. It is impossible on this side of eternity to understand the significance of the righteousness of God being imputed to the account of members of the fallen race of humanity. At best, we only see it dimly.

In the first chapter, I wrote that the idea of the **sufficiency** of Christ's sacrifice and the assurance of salvation was completely foreign to my way of thinking. It seemed too good to be true. To press that idea a little further, the sufficiency of Christ's sacrifice and the assurance of salvation will **always** be foreign to my thinking. The foundation of our faith will never rest comfortably or securely in us because salvation by grace through faith is completely contrary to natural mankind. We are always searching for ways to justify ourselves before God. Our hearts and minds tend to descend into self-condemnation, works-righteousness, and all other kinds of demonic and doubtful thoughts. It is not easy to consistently walk in faith regarding what God had done for us in Christ. It's as if you have to press the reset button every day by remembering and confessing what God has accomplished in Christ on your behalf.

PERSONAL PRAYER

Lord, I lay the whole weight of my trust on the sacrifice of Christ alone for my salvation, and I receive by faith the gift of righteousness, imputed to my account by the grace of God.

The Habit of Self-Denial

Throughout these pages, I will make repeated references to prayer and fasting, and it is generally assumed that I am referring to going without food or drink. That is indeed one example of self-denial, but far from the only application. One could conceivably fast and pray for one week at the beginning of each year and otherwise follow a lifestyle of unrestrained self-indulgence. If you only see fasting as abstaining from food for a week, it's hard not to think of it as trying to bribe God. However, if you understand fasting from food in the context of a lifestyle of self-denial for the sake of communion with God, then it takes on a higher and better meaning.

With regard to material possessions: The ethic of the modern world is to live to the full extent of one's means and beyond. For the affluent, self-denial could mean limiting your lifestyle to a level far below what you can actually afford. And it's not **just** about tithes, offerings, or generous giving. Some Christians are able to give with extraordinary generosity and still pursue a lifestyle of conspicuous consumption. It's choosing to limit one's lifestyle in order to live more simply in a world that is rapidly becoming more complicated and less contemplative; more stressful and less relational; more judgmental and less grace-filled. Deliberate simplicity is a form of self-denial that is something worth pursuing for its own sake—regardless of what one can afford to have or do.

With regard to the distraction of entertainment: In the story of Peter Pan by Scottish novelist J. M. Barrie, Peter taught young Wendy to fly by focusing on a happy thought. What is that idea that you dream about, that excites you, that you love to play with in your mind, the thoughts that help you escape from your troubles or entertain you when you're bored? Our growing addiction to instant communication, particularly via social media, has created a desperate need for seasons of fasting from it all. The American author, Sam Keen, commenting on the modern world, wrote:

> We are a generation bombarded by so many stories . . . none of which are our own. The parable of the post-modern mind is the person surrounded by a media center; three monitors giving

three sets of stories, email delivering more stories, blog posts with still more stories. The effect is that we lose the continuity of our own experiences. We become people who are written upon from the outside.[2]

Putting a more spiritual twist on his comment, Mr. Keen might well have said, "We lose the continuity of our own experience **with God**."

When you find your mind's running to forms of entertainment (good or bad) rather than running to the presence of God, ask the questions, "What is my happy thought, and why am I running from God rather than running to him?" This was the essence of Brother Lawrence's rule of discipline—to think about God as often as he could.

> **PERSONAL PRAYER**
>
> *All the vain things that charm me the most, I sacrifice them unto you. Forgive me, Lord, for running from your presence to embrace the cares and entertainments of this world.*

The Habit of Daily Surrender

At the beginning, at the end, or throughout the day, we should empty our bag of concern at the feet of Jesus. Sometimes that doesn't happen without significant struggles with our own will and desires. If, however, surrender becomes a daily habit, I don't give those wants and desires time to take root in my heart. In the parable of the sower, Jesus paints a word picture of seed planted in a field overgrown with thorns and weeds, symbolizing the "cares of this life and the desire for other things." I have a mental picture of repeatedly laying down all my desires before the Lord, only to have one jump into my pocket and follow me out the door of my prayer closet. So, I empty that desire again in his presence, but again the same thing happens. That could be a sign that I need to repent of my lingering desires or that God wants me to know that this is his plan for me. Either way, I'm going to keep laying it before him every day because no one can be truly confident about the guidance of the Holy Spirit apart from the habit of daily surrender, a habit that is expressed quite well in an old hymn by Judson W. Van DeVenter (1855–1939):

> All to Jesus I surrender,
> All to him I freely give;
> I will ever love and trust him,
> In his presence daily live.

Like Jesus said to his disciples, "If anyone would come after me, let him **deny himself** and **take up his cross daily** and follow me" (Luke 9:23).

PERSONAL PRAYER

Lord Jesus, I lay all my hopes, dreams, and desires before you, and I count all things to be loss in view of the surpassing value of knowing you (Philippians 3:8).

The Habit of Daily Confession

We cultivate his presence by surrendering unholy habits, attitudes, and words that we have allowed to dominate our inner life. Perhaps your thoughts go immediately to those involved in "significant sinning," the big five works of the flesh—sexual immorality, impurity, sensuality, idolatry, and sorcery. However, the apostle Paul's list goes on to include "enmity, strife, jealousy, fits of anger, rivalries, dissensions, divisions, envy, drunkenness, orgies, and things like these" (Galatians 5:18–21). Drunken orgies might be considered among the more significant transgressions and the latter items on that menu considered insignificant by comparison. Yet they are included in the works about which Paul repeatedly warns.

> *I warn you, as I warned you before, that those who do such things will not inherit the kingdom of God . . . But the fruit of the Spirit is love, joy, peace, patience, kindness, goodness, faithfulness, gentleness,*

self-control; against such things there is no law. And those who belong to Christ Jesus have crucified the flesh with its passions and desires.
— **GALATIANS 5:16-17, 19-24**

The apostle repeats the same exhortation to the Ephesian church that seemed to be having the same problems:

*Let no corrupting talk come out of your mouths, but only such as is good for building up, as fits the occasion, that it may give grace to those who hear. And **do not grieve the Holy Spirit of God**, by whom you were sealed for the day of redemption. Let all bitterness and wrath and anger and clamor and slander be put away from you, along with all malice.*
— **EPHESIANS 4:29-31**

Some have, over time, developed a callous or hardened heart to the person of the Spirit. Like calloused hands that are less sensitive to touch, calloused hearts increasingly become insensitive to things that quench and grieve the Holy Spirit. With regard to the Lord's vineyard, those excused attitudes and indiscretions are referred to in one of the most intimate passages of the Old Testament: "Catch the foxes for us, the little foxes that spoil the vineyards, for our vineyards are in blossom" (Song of Solomon 2:15). With foxes running wild and unrestrained throughout the vineyard, is it any wonder that one's relationship with the Holy Spirit seems stale and distant? Regular confession is one of those holy habits that cultivates a genuine communion with God—not a superficial confession but a genuine surrender and genuine awareness of our hearts' callousness to what pleases or disappoints the Holy Spirit.

PERSONAL PRAYER

Lord, I confess my sinful thoughts, words, and actions that have so frequently quenched and grieved your Holy Spirit. Soften the hardness of my heart. Open my ears to hear your voice. Quicken and empower me to do your will without hesitation.

The Habit of Meditating on God's Word

The point of our discussion in this chapter is to honor and seek the presence of God—that is, the process of preparing the soil, planting good seed, watering, fertilizing, and cultivating it so that the seed bears the fruit of the Holy Spirit in your life. One of my favorite passages is from Psalm 1:1–3:

> *Blessed is the man who walks not in the counsel of the wicked, nor stands in the way of sinners, nor sits in the seat of scoffers; but his delight is in the law of the LORD, and on his law he meditates day and night. He is like a **tree planted by streams of water that yields its fruit in its season,** and its leaf does not wither. In all that he does, he prospers.*

Unless you grew up in a farming community, you may be unaware of some concepts about preparing soil for planting. Each year soil has to be plowed and tilled, typically at a depth of about eighteen inches. Eventually, a layer of hard soil develops right beneath those eighteen inches that roots cannot penetrate. That hard layer is called a "plow pan" and requires deep plowing to break it up. Those who have been accustomed to reading the Bible at a particular depth tend to develop a kind of spiritual plow pan. The words, the narratives, and the commandments become all too familiar, and that familiarity begins to hinder the life-giving fruit of the Spirit. You begin saying to yourself, *Oh yes, I am familiar with that verse. I already know what there is to know about that passage. I have read that epistle numerous times.* If you periodically have those thoughts, perhaps it's time to dig a little deeper, time to break up the plow pan that has begun to develop in your heart by going deeper into God's word. Jesus repeatedly referred to those who were dull of hearing as having hardened hearts. Hosea prophesied about planting seeds of righteousness: "Sow for yourselves righteousness; reap steadfast love; break up your fallow ground, for it is the time to seek the LORD, that he may come and rain righteousness upon you" (Hosea 10:12).

Many employ the SOAP method, which is an acronym for Scripture, Observation, Application, and Prayer.

1. Read a passage of **Scripture** and write down the key verses.

2. Record your **observations** about the context and background, as well as the spiritual and theological implications.

3. Consider the **applications** to your life as a disciple of Jesus.

4. Turn the observations and applications into personal **prayers**. You will notice in this chapter and all the succeeding chapters that I have restated my own observations and applications as personal prayers.

This is a simple and straightforward way of meditating upon God's word. Nonetheless, I feel compelled to add a brief point of clarification. One of my favorite books on Bible study is by Dr. Gordon Fee, entitled *How to Read the Bible for All Its Worth*. The emphasis is on interpretation and application based on the context and intent of the text. In contrast, many devotional teachers (even those considered theologically conservative) emphasize using one's creative imagination. More specifically, the reader is to imagine Jesus speaking to them, walking through green pastures together, flying through the air together, or ascending above the stratosphere. They offer advice on how to sit or breathe to activate their imaginary relationship with Jesus. When the apostle Paul talked about meditation and revelation from the Holy Spirit, it was always revelational knowledge about what God has actually done for us in a historical context (Ephesians 1:16–23), not in imaginary narratives about Jesus. One Christian devotional teacher wrote, "The best overall preparation for successful meditation is the personal conviction of its importance and a staunch conviction to persevere in the practice."[3] I respectfully disagree. The best preparation for meditation as a Christian is to be firmly anchored in God's word. The apostle Paul instructed Timothy to "charge certain persons not to teach any different doctrine, nor to devote themselves to myths and endless genealogies, which promote speculations rather than the stewardship from God that is by faith" (1 Timothy 1:3–4). This was probably the source of the gnostic heresies—individuals claiming to be teachers with special revelational knowledge about the words and deeds of Jesus outside of historical context. My point is that there is a great depth of personal inspiration, revelation, and application about the mighty words and deeds of Jesus without imaginary speculations that are not anchored in truth.

PERSONAL PRAYER

Father in heaven, give me the Spirit of wisdom and revelation in the knowledge of Jesus Christ. Open the eyes of my heart that I may know what is the hope to which you have called me, what are the riches of your glorious inheritance in the saints, and what is the immeasurable greatness of your power toward me as a believer. Fill me according to the working of your great might that you worked in Christ when you raised him from the dead and seated him at your right hand in the heavenly places, far above all rule and authority and power and dominion, and above every name that is named, not only in this age but also in the one to come (Ephesians 1:17–21).

The Habit of Remembering God's Love.

Oh Lord, open the eyes of my heart that I might behold the breadth and length and height and depth of your great love for me (Ephesians 3:18). May I be consumed by your love, to the end that time in your presence is my insatiable desire.

The Habit of Holy Communion.

As I eat this meal and drink from this cup, I remember the sacrifice for my sin and the price you paid for my redemption. And in doing so, I will boldly and joyously proclaim your death and resurrection until your return (1 Corinthians 11:24–26).

The Habit of Remembering Our Desperate Need.

Lord, I lay the whole weight of my trust on the sacrifice of Christ alone for my salvation, and I receive by faith the gift of righteousness, imputed to my account by the grace of God.

The Habit of Self-Denial.

All the vain things that charm me the most, I sacrifice them unto you. Forgive me, Lord, for running from your presence to embrace the cares and entertainments of this world.

The Habit of Daily Surrender.

Lord Jesus, I lay all my hopes, dreams, and desires before you, and I count all things to be loss in view of the surpassing value of knowing you (Philippians 3:8).

The Habit of Daily Confession.

Lord, I confess my sinful thoughts, words, and actions that have so frequently quenched and grieved your Holy Spirit. Soften the hardness of my heart. Open my ears to hear your voice. Quicken and empower me to do your will without hesitation.

The Habit of Meditating on God's Word.

Father in heaven, give me the Spirit of wisdom and revelation in the knowledge of Jesus Christ. Open the eyes of my heart that I may know what is the hope to which you have called me, what are the riches of your glorious inheritance in the saints, and what is the immeasurable greatness of your power toward me as a believer. Fill me according to the working of your great might that you worked in Christ when you raised him from the dead and seated him at your right hand in the heavenly places, far above all rule and authority and power and dominion, and above every name that is named, not only in this age but also in the one to come (Ephesians 1:17–21).

CHAPTER FIVE

CORPORATE PRAYER

"And now, Lord, look upon their threats and grant to your servants to continue to speak your word with all boldness, while you stretch out your hand to heal, and signs and wonders are performed through the name of your holy servant Jesus." And when they had prayed, the place in which they were gathered together was shaken, and they were all filled with the Holy Spirit and continued to speak the word of God with boldness.

— ACTS 4:29–31

There was a tremendous move of the Spirit in the early days of Victory. So many things happened that it's hard to get your head around the story—extraordinary faith and boldness combined with such an acute sense of desperation. I was aware of Scripture passages that described our neediness. Jesus is the vine and apart from him "you can do nothing" (John 15:5). "It is the Spirit who gives life; the flesh is no help at all" (John 6:63). I was no biblical scholar, but I knew (at least theologically and personally) that we should put our trust in the power of God, not in our own abilities, efforts, or resources. The stories from the first three years of Victory were about students who felt that sense of total desperation at the very core of their lives but who had, nonetheless, been transformed and empowered by the Holy Spirit to believe that all things were not only possible but to be expected.

I know that sounds like a senior citizen reminiscing about the good ole days. The good news, however, is that the same Holy Spirit is inspiring and empowering that same kind of faith, vision, and desperation in generation after generation of new believers. It seems to me that our sense of desperation and unbridled expectation continues in proportion to our vision and commitment to go into all the world and make disciples. As a leader in Victory today, I am simply trying to fan the flames of those who are already on fire for God by equipping them to win souls and make disciples of Jesus. I frequently remind myself of the apostle Paul's exhortation, "Do not quench the Spirit" (1 Thessalonians 5:19).

As I said, so many things happened, but they didn't **just** happen. Almost every story worth telling was a direct answer to passionate, desperate, and faith-filled prayer—much of it corporate prayer. It would be impossible to mention every significant event that was a result of corporate prayer because many of the important acts of supernatural protection, provision, and guidance are acts of divine intervention of which we are unaware. Nonetheless, I have listed six answers to corporate prayer that have created and perpetuated the tradition of prayer and fasting in our church. It is certainly not a complete list, and I'm sure others will point to different examples. These are, at least in my mind, our top six.

Corporate Prayer for the Nations

Students caught the vision of going into all the world to preach the gospel and make disciples through corporate prayer. One of the earliest traditions of Victory U-Belt was the students interceding for nations one by one, laying their hands upon a giant National Geographic world map plastered on the wall of our student center. The significance of the prayer "Here I am! Send me" (Isaiah 6:8), voiced by so many new believers, was that almost none of those early disciples had ever been off the island of Luzon where Metro Manila is or had ever been on an airplane. Looking back from our current perspective, intercessory prayer for the nations with our hands on the big map was among the most significant events in the history of our church. Those corporate prayer meetings laid the foundation of the young church. Every time we gathered in our facility, that map on the wall would stir our hearts, reminding us that "God so loved the world, that he gave his only Son, that whoever believes in him should not perish but have eternal life" (John 3:16). The Lord seems to have been answering those prayers throughout the last thirty-seven years as teams of church planters have left the Philippines and gone into all the world preaching the gospel and making disciples. Besides the churches planted throughout the Philippines, as of 2021, our missionaries have established churches in 38 other nations—19 in Asia, 8 in the Middle East, 4 in Europe, 5 in North America, and 2 in Oceania.

Corporate Prayer for Divine Wisdom and Guidance

In chapter 6, I briefly tell the story of the formulation of our discipleship strategy. We began desperately seeking God's wisdom on more effective ways to make disciples. The process was born out of an extended season of intense prayer among our leaders, has been fine-tuned regularly, and continues to engage unbelievers with the gospel—establishing them in the faith, equipping them to minister, and empowering them to make disciples. In *WikiChurch,* Pastor Steve Murrell describes the strategy that has been applied in both Victory and Every Nation. But more than this discipleship strategy, prayer has been responsible for the growth of Victory.

Corporate Prayer and Unprecedented Provision

In the mid–1990s, our church was planning to make our first property purchase. Not knowing that the Asian financial crisis of 1997 was looming, we decided to make the purchase in cash. Pastor Steve Murrell recalls God's providence behind this:

> I have been a believer since I was sixteen years old and a pastor/preacher for thirty years. In all those years I can count only three times when God has spoken to me with undeniable clarity. The first time was a sense that Deborah was to be my wife. Fortunately, she agreed. The third time I "know that I know" God spoke to me was several years later. It had to do with the first church property we bought in Manila. I had no idea what was about to happen

to the Philippine economy, but I just knew God said we were to avoid debt and pay cash. Soon afterward the Philippine peso crashed, and interest rates soared to 30 percent. Had we used debt to purchase that property, we would have been in big trouble.[1]

"Big trouble" was an understatement. Had we borrowed the money on those terms, it would have hampered every expansion initiative and all the support of compassion ministries for many years.

In 2000, sixteen years after Victory had been established in U-Belt, Victory congregations in Metro Manila had grown both numerically and financially. Our offering baskets no longer just jingled with coins as in the early days. We were contemplating the construction of a facility in Bonifacio Global City that would serve as a regional office for Every Nation. The building we envisioned would cost millions of pesos on a one-hectare property leased long-term from the government. Banks were willing to finance our new facility with a variable interest rate mortgage.

Having been spared by God from a debt trap in 1997, Pastor Steve called for seven days of prayer and fasting for God's provision. We knew we didn't want to get into debt for this project. Our faith was to pay for what was needed in cash. God met us at our point of faith, and every need was miraculously met with his provision. Within two years, we had raised the full cost of the new building.

Corporate Prayer for Protection

In 2003, two years after the attack that destroyed the twin towers of the World Trade Center in New York, a window of opportunity opened for missionaries to enter Kabul, Afghanistan. As originally recounted by Dr. Jun Escosar in *A Bible and a Passport*, teams from our Every Nation churches in Asia, Europe, and the United States were eager to go. From Asia alone, over 100 had volunteered to go, and that alone was far too many. Asian leaders had to cut the number down to seventeen, like Gideon and the armies of Israel.

Jim Laffoon had a prophetic word on a conference call with members of the Every Nation International Apostolic Team (IAT). I remember the call and Jim's sense of urgency about intercession. "The devil will try to kill Every Nation leaders in an Asian nation. I'm not sure which nation, but you should watch and pray for the next three months." We began praying regularly. Soon, the burden to intercede for the team spread to many of our local churches' regular prayer gatherings. A lot of the team in Afghanistan were Filipinos, so the Victory churches in the Philippines prayed with added concern. Before long, a call to prayer was sent out to all Every Nation churches. Intense prayer for the team in Kabul seemed to be Holy Spirit-inspired.

The team arrived on April 6 and began working with a Christian NGO based in Kabul, and with several members of our Every Nation churches in North America who were already there. Two months into their stay, visiting intercessors had warned the team that they should be on their guard. At the same time, both American and British embassies issued warnings that Taliban fighters were planning a four-day bloodbath against coalition forces. This was more than enough to put our team on high alert and motivate them to engage in some serious intercessory prayer. On the third day of the Taliban's campaign, several team members were leaving the compound in Central Kabul for the eight-kilometer trip to the university. In the last van were an Afghan driver, three Americans, one German, and two Filipinos, including Mel Techo, the leader of the Filipino team. About three kilometers away from the university, Mel noticed that two men on a motorcycle had aligned with their van. Seconds later, the rider in the back pulled the pin on a Russian fragmentation grenade and threw it into the front passenger window of their van. The grenade did not explode, and Mel retrieved the grenade and threw it out.

After the grenade incident, the students and faculty members' attitudes toward the team changed. Muslims regard miracles with high esteem, and so they concluded that the hand of God had protected and covered the team that day. Mel helped disciple four students in Afghanistan—the relative of the Taliban leader, two who had recently finished their law studies, and one who now works at the US Library at Kabul University. As the story made its way through the churches, it became like one of the twelve memorial stones Joshua gathered to remind the children of Israel that God was with them and had parted the waters of the Jordan River (Joshua 4:1–7).

Corporate Prayer as a Witness to Unbelievers

Prayer is a vital part of reaching out to unbelievers. Church members who want to start Victory groups are encouraged to meet for a few weeks to pray and intercede with others for specific friends and family who they can invite to the Victory group. We also rely on God's wisdom and insight as we begin helping others follow Jesus and even go through *One2One*, a discipleship material designed to engage and establish new believers.

As Victory groups meet every week, family and friends are invited to join and we take time to pray for their needs. We've heard of many miracles as a testimony of God's power through prayers. Answers to prayer, particularly as a witness to unbelievers, seem to happen with surprising frequency. Faith is contagious. For those in Victory groups, including some that are led by relatively new believers, stepping out in faith and seeing God do miracles builds their faith and leads many others to Christ.

Corporate Prayer and Fasting

In 2016, the Every Nation IAT met to consider what traditions had served to unify the church across the five Every Nation regions worldwide. IAT members offered several suggestions, including holding the Every Nation World Conference every three years. Seasons of prayer and fasting were already a tradition in Victory and Every Nation churches in the Philippines, Asia, and the Middle East, as well as some of our churches in North America. Eventually, someone suggested, "Since we engage in seasons of prayer and fasting at various times throughout the year, why don't we all do it together at least once a year?" The idea resonated with all the leaders, and in 2017 we held the first annual week of prayer, fasting, and consecration together with Every Nation churches around the world.

Jim Laffoon wrote the first prayer-guide booklet entitled *Knowing God*, followed by *In Christ* (2018), *Great Faith* (2019), *Amazing Grace* (2020), and *Awesome God* (2021). Prayer and fasting continues to be an annual tradition among Every Nation churches.

Back To The Philippines

After graduating from UVA's Darden School of Business, my student visa allowed me to spend one additional year doing my practical training in the United States. However, I was reminded that God's "hidden hand of providence," as it is sometimes called, was still at work in my life. A multinational bank recruiter came to the UVA campus one day to interview me and my friend Chito Zulueta for positions in their consumer banking division in Manila. Chito and I were two of five Filipinos in our class and were also both discipled in the church. A few days later, the bank called to say that Chito and I were given job offers in (of all places) Makati, the business district of Metro Manila and the site of Victory's second church plant. So, I guess I could say, like Pastor Steve, I didn't come back to the Philippines because I received a specific calling from God. While Pastor Steve got a call from Pastor Rice, I got a call through this bank.

Generally speaking, prophetic words given by believers in a church or Christian context are things that you hide in your heart. Rather than causing you to pursue a career choice based on a particular prophecy, they usually serve to confirm the leading of the Holy Spirit. People commonly say, "Oh, yes. I remember now that prophetic word I was given." That was the case when the angel spoke to the mother of Jesus about her miraculous conception (Luke 2:19) and when Jesus foretold Peter's betrayal (Mark 14:26–31). Peter remembered Jesus' words when the rooster crowed the second time (Mark 14:71–72). At the outpouring of the Holy Spirit at Pentecost, the apostles remembered Jesus saying, "John baptized with water, but you will be baptized with the Holy Spirit" (Acts 11:15–16). Then there was the prophecy concerning the fate of the apostle Paul delivered by the prophet Agabus (Acts 21:10–11). The prophetic words came back to each of them as a confirmation that God was with them in dark times, glorious times, or times when they had no clear sense of God's leading. Having accepted the offer from the financial institution that effectively rendered moot the time I had planned to spend in the US preparing for my career, a prophetic word about returning to my home country came rushing back into my memory. It was the first of three prophetic confirmations that I was indeed following God's leading, even though he was leading me in directions I had never intended to go.

I returned to the Philippines in June of 1987, three years after the initial U-Belt outreach amid student protests that eventually led to the People Power Revolution toppling the Marcos regime in 1986. When I finally arrived in Manila, I stayed with my parents and siblings, whom I hadn't seen for two years, and immediately reported for work at the bank head office. Before leaving our church in Charlottesville, I had gotten the address and phone number of the church in the Philippines connected to Maranatha. I was looking forward to attending the church, not knowing it was Victory. The first Sunday I could, I decided to attend the afternoon worship service in U-Belt. The moment I stepped into the service, I was immediately caught up in the fire and passion of hundreds of students praising God. Even though the place was sweaty due to lack of air conditioning, the young people were not at all deterred from expressing their love for God. I didn't get to meet Pastor Steve until after the service, but I was impressed that his message was not only foundational but also practical. He warmly greeted me as someone who had come from the same church family in the US, but our encounter was brief. He had to attend to many other people.

The next Sunday, Chito and I joined the morning service this time in Makati, and that was when we were welcomed by Pastor Steve and Joey and Marie Bonifacio, one of the few married couples in the early years of the church. When the praise and worship started, I felt the same tangible presence of God as in the U-Belt service, but there was also a sense of genuine spiritual community. At that point, I felt that I had finally arrived home—not just to my country but to my spiritual family.

In the next few months, as I got into the routine of work and church participation, I began to feel a sense of responsibility to start serving more in the Makati congregation, whether in discipleship, in the prayer meetings, or by prophesying in the worship services. I had never prophesied in Charlottesville and hesitated at first in Victory, but in time I felt prompted to do so. I felt such a strong stirring of the Spirit, and Pastor Steve encouraged me and others to speak. I was impressed by the passion and zeal of the pastors and evangelists at Victory and respected them even though they were slightly younger than me, which mattered in a hierarchical culture like the Philippines.

What I did not know then was that in less than a year, I would join the Victory staff with Steve and Deborah Murrell, Tom Bouvier, Jun Escosar, Ferdie Cabiling, and some other campus missionaries. When I was still wrestling in early 1988 with the Holy Spirit regarding my calling to vocational ministry, an itinerant prophet, John Rohrer, came through Manila. This was not my first encounter with a prophetic minister, and given my hesitations with God's calling, I had mixed emotions about his visit. I was excited and hoping to "get a word from God" and, at the same time, a bit reluctant to hear what that prophetic word might be and where it would lead. I understood that it was only to confirm what I had already been sensing. I knew what the Holy Spirit was calling me to do; I just needed the courage to follow.

I still aspired to work for a high corporate management position and perhaps take a government role in the future as an elected official. On previous occasions, I would make casual comments about my dream to become a senator one day. I knew it was a noble task to those who are called to it. However, as the sense of God's calling began to grow in me, talking about my political dreams just didn't seem as exciting anymore. It had lost its luster, yet it was hard for me to put on the altar. In retrospect, the current path of the corporate world and a future stint in government would have allowed me to stay in my comfort zone, and it was difficult to let go of.

I shared my conflicting career visions with Pastor Steve—that I felt called to the ministry but still had the desire to serve as an elected official.

I'm not sure whether or not I used the term "senator." It was beginning to sound a bit pompous even when I said it to myself. Characteristically, he listened carefully, asked a few questions, and delivered his opinion in as few words as clarity required.

"Manny," he finally said, "if you're a senator, you're only one person. But if you're a pastor, you can disciple senators, businessmen, government leaders, and everyone else."

"Okay," I replied. "That makes sense."

However, it really only made sense with a considerable leap of faith. Even after four years, Victory was still a pretty ragtag group of young people, students, and a growing number of twenty-somethings. How many senators, businessmen, and government officials would join Victory, and how many would want to be discipled by us?

When John Rohrer finally arrived, he started prophesying over several people gathered for a leaders' meeting, and when it was my turn, he declared that I was called to be a prophet to the nations. I wasn't sure what prophetic ministers did. Were they supposed to go to the office, clock in, and start prophesying? Probably not. Even though the prophetic ministry was hard to define, the word from John Rohrer was a confirmation of what I had been feeling for several months—that I was called to the ministry. So, in April of 1988, I gave my notice, left my job at the bank, and became the associate pastor at Victory Makati, getting a salary that was around half of what I had been receiving.

Personal Lessons on Corporate Prayer

We should come into God's presence faithfully and commune with him reverently.

As the new associate pastor at Victory Makati, I began leading a weekly prayer meeting. Whether that was an assigned duty or simply an assumed responsibility, I do not remember. Seasoned evangelists like Tom Bouvier, Jun Escosar, and Ferdie Cabiling were leaders I greatly admired. They seemed to have such a clear understanding of their roles and responsibilities.

I began trying to organize a corporate prayer meeting, I think partly because I didn't know what else to do.

At the church in Charlottesville, Virginia, I had learned a lot about individual devotional prayer, primarily from Jim Lowen. Jim was a captain in the United States Army and a no-nonsense kind of guy. If discipleship is learning the discipline of a teacher, my friend Chito and I got a full dose of it from Captain Lowen. He invited us to join him for prayer once a week at 6:00 a.m. The first Wednesday morning, we staggered into Captain Lowen's apartment, barely awake and with plans to go back to bed when the captain was done with us. In contrast, that morning and every Wednesday morning after that, Jim welcomed us in his perfectly pressed military uniform, clean-shaven and ready for the day. He had no intention of returning to bed. After a quick greeting, the captain wasted little time. He went down on his knees and began communing with God. That first morning, I didn't know if we should salute or respond to his invitation to begin our prayer time with a loud "Sir, yes, sir." But he was expecting neither. As we entered this new world of discipline in prayer, we learned to pray each week on our knees.

Chito and I were struck by the discipline and character of Captain James Lowen. He made an unforgettable impression on two young Filipino graduate students for the few months that he taught us about prayer. I think about him each time I hear Pastor Steve and other Victory pastors refer to an early version of why Victory exists: "To honor God and advance His kingdom by making disciples, training leaders, and planting churches in the Philippines, Asia, and the world."

PERSONAL PRAYER

Forgive me, Lord, for the times I have entered your presence so casually or offered up my petitions half-heartedly. Even as I am invited to address you as a child to a father, may I not dishonor you through presumptuous prayers or forget that you are a God who dwells in unapproachable light (1 Timothy 6:16).

It's not about the numbers.

Prayer is what undergirds and empowers every aspect of what we do, both individually and corporately. My desire to develop a culture and tradition of corporate prayer at Victory Makati was genuine but not very well thought out. It was one thing for two students to drop by Captain Lowen's once a week in the small town of Charlottesville. Leading an early-morning corporate prayer meeting in Metro Manila each week was a much greater challenge. In the early 1990s, rush hour traffic in a metropolis of over eight million people, unreliable public transportation, and the fact that few people in our congregation owned cars made a 6:00 a.m. prayer meeting hard to attend—something that had never occurred to me. Consequently, my earliest efforts at motivating and organizing corporate prayer were not that successful. Only a handful of intercessors showed up every week. However, our monthly prayer meeting in the evening was attended by 20–25 percent of the Victory Makati congregation. I concluded that the low turnout of our morning prayer gatherings was more a practical issue about transportation and work schedules than the lack of commitment of our members to pray.

From what seemed to be an unsuccessful attempt at organizing corporate prayer meetings, I learned that it is not about the numbers. A lot of people participating in a prayer meeting does not necessarily mean our demands are validated by a huge mob at the gates of heaven. Prayers by a precious few or a great many do not inform God about anything he doesn't already know. It is more for our benefit and our faith that he welcomes our petitions. Corporate prayer could be understood in the context of Matthew 18:19–20, ". . . if two of you agree on earth about anything they ask, it will be done for them by my Father in heaven. For where two or three are gathered in my name, there am I among them." Many of our most significant answers to prayers have been the result of corporate prayer gatherings of only a handful of intercessors.

PERSONAL PRAYER

Oh Lord, forgive me for assuming that answers to prayer are dependent on the number of people praying rather than the power of agreement. Sanctify and enable me to keep my eyes firmly fixed on you, knowing that as we faithfully intercede, whether by many or by few (1 Samuel 14:6), deliverance will come.

God calls individuals to intercession but not necessarily to lead organized prayer.

Within the Every Nation global family of churches, there are a relatively small number of individuals and couples who have a distinct calling to prayer—hopefully, a group of intercessors in every congregation. Joey and Marie Bonifacio, Mary Malinao, Joel Barrios, Hedy Ner, Chelo Gemina, Rean and Tess Tirol, and several others in the earlier years played vital roles through their prayers in birthing churches, protecting missionaries, and opening doors for the gospel. Then there are the unknown individuals who consistently stand in the gap for God's kingdom to come on earth as it is in heaven. That last group of unknowns might be the most numerous, because people with a calling to intense intercession are often the ones who are least likely to stand out as individuals with the gift of leadership. They are a lot (perhaps far more) like Jesus who consistently went off to pray without inviting others to come along. The disciples were often left wondering, *What happened to Jesus? Where did he go?* Jesus was off alone talking with the Father. Dedicated intercessors are all about praying, often with little or no concern about organizing the prayer meeting. To put it another way, these called and Spirit-empowered intercessors do not need an officially sanctioned prayer meeting to motivate them to pray. Just because people are deeply committed to prayer doesn't mean they are to organize and lead the prayer meeting. It's often the last thing they desire to do and possibly the last thing they are likely to be successful doing.

At the same time, some not only feel a great burden to pray but also have the burden to organize and encourage prayer in our churches. Jim Laffoon, Mary Malinao, Jojo Henson, Edgar Gorre, and Erwin Ramos are a few examples. Bob Perry organized and led the intercession for unbelievers each night during the initial outreach meetings at Victory U-Belt in June of 1984. Decades later, Bob still has an enormous impact on organizing and leading intercessory prayer in greater Nashville, Tennessee. I aspire to follow in the footsteps of these great intercessors and prayer organizers. What I have learned is that within the ministry of intercession, there are a variety of motivational giftings. We need to encourage everyone in prayer while allowing them to run in their own lanes.

PERSONAL PRAYER

Lord, thank you for those who have responded to the call to intercede for others and those you will call, even without an organized prayer meeting. You know what the Spirit has called each person to do. If we have great movements of prayer in our church, it will be because of the inspiration and empowering of your Spirit.

God is not hard of hearing.

I've been in many prayer meetings where believers cried out with great passion or desperation. At times it can become a shouting match, as if God were inattentive or hard of hearing. However, you can't measure the effectiveness or the intensity of a corporate prayer meeting by the volume of the petitioners. This reality was reinforced in my mind by one of Dr. Jun Escosar's missionary adventures. For many years, Jun served as the missions director of Every Nation Asia and is now the president of Every Nation Seminary. In 1996, Jun was on an exploratory mission trip to Ho Chi Minh City, Vietnam. He recalls this story in his book, *A Bible and a Passport.* The organizers arranged for him to teach for several days at a house church. Arriving at the designated meeting place, a person behind the door watched through a small peephole to control the flow of believers arriving and departing. That process seemed to work well—so well that Jun expected only a handful of Christians at the meeting. When he was finally allowed by the monitors to come in, he was shocked to see over 200 believers packed like sardines in the living room. One of the lookouts spotted over a dozen policemen launching a highly coordinated raid just outside their meeting place, apparently raiding another building. The lookout signaled for everyone to be quiet and intercede for those in the house being raided. Were the police to barge in, Jun and another foreigner were cautioned not to speak but blend in with the locals. Perhaps the police were searching for their meeting. But by God's grace, after a moment of this silent intercession, the police went back to their cars and left. Many years later, Jun recounted, "It's truly impossible to describe the intensity or the power of those prayers, even though their combined voices were no louder than a whisper."[2]

> **PERSONAL PRAYER**
>
> *Teach me to be sensitive to your Spirit in times of prayer. If I shout as loud as I can or if I wait on the Spirit in silence, govern my heart and my voice that I might be as an instrument yielded to you.*

Small groups of intercessors can grow into world-changing movements.

Several notable examples come to mind.

The 100-year Moravian Prayer Meeting: At the Sunday service on August 13, 1727, as they were celebrating the Lord's Supper, Moravian refugees experienced what could only be called a Pentecostal outpouring of the Holy Spirit. Their hearts were set on fire as the participants were all filled with the Spirit. Those who were not yet believers immediately accepted Christ as their Lord and Savior. There was an overwhelming sense of the presence of the Holy Spirit, evidenced by a general conviction of sin, a burning love for Christ and one another, and the manifestation of the gifts of the Spirit. Members continued to meet in their small groups, confessing their sins and praying for individuals to be healed of infirmities.

On August 27, two weeks after the initial outpouring of the Spirit, twenty-four men and twenty-four women pledged to spend one hour each day in round-the-clock prayer. The renewal that continued through the next four months came to be known among the Moravians as the Golden Summer of 1727. Others joined in the daily intercession, and over the following decades, one generation after another enlisted in the 24/7 scheduled intercession that continued uninterrupted for over 100 years. In the 1700s, going as missionaries into all the world was unprecedented. As impressive as the Moravians' 100-year prayer watch was, equally (and perhaps even more) significant was that their commitment to pray was combined with their willingness to go. The years 1732–1742 are unmatched when it comes to the history of Christian missionaries. Out of a Moravian community of 600, over 70 responded to the call to missions by 1742. By 1760, no fewer than 226 missionaries had been sent out from Herrnhut. By the time William Carey published his little seventy-eight-page booklet, *An Enquiry into the Obligations of Christians to Use Means for the Conversion of the Heathens* (a.k.a. *The Enquiry*) in 1792, 2,158 Moravians had already answered the call to serve overseas.

The Fulton Street Prayer Meeting: Jeremiah Lanphier found that his time spent in prayer brought him the most peace and resolve, and he determined to start a weekly noon prayer meeting for businessmen to take advantage of the hour when businesses were closed for lunch. The handbill he had printed read: "Wednesday prayer meeting from 12 to 1 o'clock. Stop 5, 10, or 20 minutes, or the whole time, as your time admits." On September 23, 1857, he set up a signboard in front of the church. No one came to the appointed room, and Lanphier prayed by himself for thirty minutes. At 12:30 another man joined him, four more by the end of the hour. The next week there were twenty men, forty the following week. In October the prayer meetings became daily; in January 1858 a second room had to be used simultaneously; by February, a third. By then as many as twenty noon prayer meetings were being held elsewhere in the city. In mid-March, Burton's Theatre, capable of holding 3,000, was crowded for a prayer meeting. By the end of March, every downtown New York church and public hall was filled, and 10,000 were gathering daily for prayer.

Meetings sprang up in other parts of the city. It is estimated that there were 10,000 conversions in Philadelphia in 1858. One denomination received 3,000 new members. In Boston, a prayer meeting was held in historic Old South Church and in Park Street Church. At least 150 Massachusetts towns were touched by the revival, with 5,000 conversions before the end of March. The Boston correspondent of a Washington newspaper wrote that religion was the chief concern in many cities and towns of New England.[3]

The Great Experiment at Asbury College: In February 1970, one student at Asbury College in Wilmore, Kentucky, became deeply concerned for the blessing of God on campus. So she gathered a group around her, and they started praying. Six students came together in what they called "the great experiment." At the end of thirty days of prayer, each of those six invited five others. Now there were six groups of six getting up every morning for thirty minutes in prayer. On January 31, they led the chapel service with thirty-six of them on the platform, sharing what the great experiment had done for them. There was a commitment slip on every seat, inviting students to commit themselves to become a part of a group of six, who would engage in this experiment for thirty days. A week later there was an outpouring of the Holy Spirit in the Tuesday morning chapel service that went on day and night for seven days and sparked a great spiritual awakening in churches and campuses all across North America.[4]

PERSONAL PRAYER

Lord, pour out your Spirit upon us. We repent and turn to you that our sins may be blotted out and that times of refreshing may come from your presence (Acts 3:19–20).

• • •

The outpouring of the Holy Spirit results in the birthing of movements of prayer and fasting, as well as repentance and conversion experiences. These do not happen by our own determination or willpower, but by responding to rather than resisting the promptings of the Spirit.

In our own time, I believe that the current COVID-19 crisis we are facing is giving birth to a Spirit-inspired prayer movement throughout all of the churches and campus ministries in Every Nation. Though many are more experienced in writing and in prayer, I am privileged to have been asked to give expression to this endeavor.

We should come into God's presence faithfully and commune with him reverently.

Forgive me, Lord, for the times I have entered your presence so casually or offered up my petitions half-heartedly. Even as I am invited to address you as a child to a father, may I not dishonor you through presumptuous prayers or forget that you are a God who dwells in unapproachable light (1 Timothy 6:16).

It's not about the numbers.

Oh Lord, forgive me for assuming that our answers to prayer are dependent on the number of people praying rather than the power of agreement. Sanctify and enable me to keep my eyes firmly fixed on you, knowing that as we faithfully intercede, whether by many or by few (1 Samuel 14:6), deliverance will come.

God calls individuals to intercession but not necessarily to lead organized prayer.

Lord, thank you for those who have responded to the call to intercede for others and those you will call, even without an organized prayer meeting. You know what the Spirit has called each person to do. If we have great movements of prayer in our church, it will be because of the inspiration and empowering of your Spirit.

God is not hard of hearing.

Teach me to be sensitive to your Spirit in times of prayer. If I shout as loud as I can or if I wait on the Spirit in silence, govern my heart and my voice that I might be as an instrument yielded to you.

Small groups of intercessors can grow into world-changing movements

Lord, pour out your Spirit upon us. We repent and turn to you that our sins may be blotted out and that times of refreshing may come from your presence (Acts 3:19–20).

CHAPTER SIX

PRAYING AND PLANTING

Neither he who plants nor he who waters is anything, but only God who gives the growth.

—1 CORINTHIANS 3:7

Growing in faith seldom occurs without simultaneous growth in our prayer lives, and vice versa. It's the answers to prayer that grow our faith—even if we have to persevere in prayer for a long time, and even if we only become aware of God's guidance and provision in retrospect. In some ways, that kind of growth in our faith is more solid and more enduring than immediate answers to our every request.

In this chapter and the next, I outline some of the ways we can effectively pray for missionaries and church planters, whether they are going to establish underground churches in creative-access nations or plant churches in the Bible belt of the American south. However, before I get to my prayer points, I want to briefly discuss a few important things we learned about ministry expansion through church planting in the first decade of Victory. Most of it followed an early-church pattern. It was passionate, sacrificial, and visionary, though not seemingly strategic.

. . .

My primary window to the world is as one of the leaders of Victory in the Philippines. That is the context with which I talk about prayer, fasting, and consecration. It is, however, important to understand the broader context. Victory is only one part of the Every Nation global family of churches and campus ministries. Expansion priorities and reproduction strategies have evolved in each region of the world according to several factors, including spiritual strongholds, openness to the gospel, and the strength of the initial church plant in a region or nation. Concerning the number of church plants, this is not a competition, and we don't keep score. It's also not a very level playing field. An Every Nation church in a creative-access nation with fifty members is perhaps as numerically significant as a 3,000-member church in the Philippines, South Africa, or the United States. In the first decade (1984–1994), Victory planted three congregations in Metro Manila: two that were growing in a healthy manner, and one that wasn't. Our original congregation also planted churches in thirteen cities and towns outside Metro Manila. The evolution of how Victory planted churches in that first decade had several stages.

Good Harvest

Victory in the University Belt was the first church established by the American team of short-term missionaries in June of 1984. The initiative began in 1982 when Pastor Rice Broocks led a student, Al Manamtam, to Christ during an evangelistic outreach on the campus of the University of Southern California. Always looking for expansion opportunities, Rice asked Al where he was from. "Hawaii," he said, "but my parents are from the Philippines."

"One day, let's go there," was Rice's reply.

Al probably thought that was the beginning and the end of the Philippines mission idea. However, that was one of his first encounters with Rice Broocks, and Al probably didn't understand how predisposed Rice was to thinking and acting as if all things were possible. Two years later, in June 1984, Rice was staring at a world map when he felt the Holy Spirit say, "Go to Manila." The next thing he did was to call his old roommate, Steve Murrell, who had been serving as a **campus missionary** at Mississippi State University for less than a year. Rice quickly recruited a team of summer missionaries, the majority of them college students, and one month later the team landed in Manila.

The University Belt in Manila has over thirty colleges, universities, and vocational schools, with more than 360,000 students today. It has the highest concentration of students in the nation. A few of the largest universities are the Far Eastern University, San Beda University, the University of the East, and the University of Santo Tomas (the oldest university in the Philippines, founded in 1612). These students came from all over the archipelago, representing the diverse socio-economic strata of our society. There was indeed a harvest of newly saved Filipinos after one month, but not so plentiful that one could have ever expected the growth that has occurred in the succeeding decades. The team of sixty American missionaries was (by the power of the Holy Spirit) responsible for birthing a church of 160 Filipino believers. Good results, but not something they'll write about in church history books. Pastor Steve and Deborah volunteered to stay an extra month to continue making disciples and following up with new believers. It would be difficult to find a better example of the importance of early discipleship to establish enduring biblical foundations. That was especially true given that the new Filipino believers would have to take over after only a month.

In the New Testament, the apostle Paul and his team also birthed a church and left it in the care of appointed elders at Lystra (Acts 14:23) and in Crete (Titus 1:5). These quickly appointed leaders were indeed new to the Christian faith. However, they were most probably deeply versed in the Old Testament and already leaders in the synagogues—very different from the new believers of the U-Belt outreach.

Unproven Leadership

The leaders of the mission organization that had sent the American team were already asking themselves, "We know about Rice Broocks, but who is this Steve Murrell, and why should we think that he can lead a church?" But Steve had been a member of the campus ministry at Mississippi State University for years and was more ready to lead than anyone knew. Thankfully, Rice and Walter Walker went to bat for the young and inexperienced campus missionary from a little college town in Starkville, Mississippi.

Concerning ministry strategy, my understanding was that Pastor Steve was focused on U-Belt as the primary mission field of the new church. At that time, our twenty-five-year-old cofounder already had his hands full with hundreds of students in the church, with only a few years of full-time campus ministry experience tucked under his belt. He could have easily spent the rest of his life making disciples among the hordes of students in that university hub.

Nervous Parents

Eventually, several students from more exclusive private schools like De La Salle University and Assumption College started getting saved and filled with the Holy Spirit. Some of those students eventually got married and became pastors, and quite a few are still part of our church more than thirty years later. In 1988, however, the affluent parents of these students would not allow them to go regularly into the crime-ridden areas of U-Belt. While most crimes were petty, they were numerous enough to build a reputation of danger in the minds of parents. The students from these exclusive schools started asking to meet in a safer place that was acceptable to their parents. In response, we began a weekly Bible study in Makati, which quickly grew into a local church. That's where I got my start as an associate pastor in 1988. Makati was almost as community-oriented as U-Belt was student-oriented.

Unhealthy Fast Growth

At Victory Makati, our church was made up of students, young professionals, families, and grandparents. The church grew over the next four years to the point that we were at maximum capacity at the Makati Sports Club. We began looking for another venue. Pastor Steve explains our next move, which turned out to be our first "unplanned" church-planting endeavor:

What seemed to be a great church-planting opportunity turned into a struggle that revealed some serious cracks in our ministry strategy. I received a call from . . . the owner of the Star Complex theater in the Shangri-La Mall. The former movie theater had been converted into a one-thousand-seat facility designed for stage plays, musicals, and concerts. The man was told, "Call Steve Murrell. He'll start a church anywhere."[1]

We asked a group of Victory Makati members to begin attending a worship service at the Shangri-La Mall where I would lead worship. Before we realized what was happening, the service had quickly grown to almost a thousand. At the U-Belt outreach meetings, Pastor Rice had periodically told visitors from other churches, "We're glad you came, but please do not come back to these meetings. We simply don't have enough seats. We are here to reach lost Filipino students." Those reached at the U-Belt outreach were almost all new believers. In Makati, we were still making disciples of students, families, and children. But at the Shangri-La Mall, we had become an attractional church, drawing all kinds of people even without intentionally reaching out to them. Spectators, critics, celebrities, and Christians who were simply looking for a new worship experience came. Our church was growing fast, mostly from transferees. But even then, a lot of great disciples and leaders came from that initiative—many who still serve with us today.

Fasting, Prayer, and Rededication

We eventually discontinued that afternoon service, transferred to two other temporary venues to launch a morning and an afternoon service, and engaged in some deep soul-searching over the next year. We knew we were called to make disciples, train leaders, and plant churches, but even with membership of almost 1,000, we didn't have the strategy to make it work. We entered into a season of intense prayer and fasting, observing and learning from what other churches were doing, and repeated trial and error. This eventually brought forth our clearly defined discipleship strategy—we engage culture and community, we establish biblical foundations, we equip believers for ministry, and we empower disciples to make disciples.

We also reaffirmed our calling and commitment to make disciples and train leaders among the students of Metro Manila. We had never abandoned that vision, but the Shangri-La Mall experience intensified our focus. Perhaps one of the "cracks" in our ministry strategy was that in our anxiousness to find meeting facilities, we were predisposed to proceed through any open door. That was a lesson I would need to remember in our next church-planting initiative.

• • •

By the mid-1990s, we had a pretty clear sense of mission—preach the gospel, make disciples, and train leaders. Though we've continually tweaked, tinkered with, and adjusted our discipleship strategy, this has been the basis for our growth for over twenty-five years. In the first decade, we were not as strategic in our expansion efforts, but we were getting our bearings with regard to discipleship. We established new Victory congregations as people from distant campuses and communities became disciples and as venues became available. That was the driving force that led us to establish congregations in Makati and Shangri-La. This does not necessarily signify a lack of planning. It is more characteristic of expansions led by the Holy Spirit.

In the early church, that same kind of thing was happening. The gospel spread and congregations formed organically without any kind of strategic plan other than by the Holy Spirit opening doors for the gospel. Churches were established as a natural result of visitors traveling to and from Jerusalem: when new believers were scattered all over Asia Minor fleeing from the persecution of Saul (Acts 8:1); when Philip was visited by an angel with instructions to leave the exploding revival in Samaria and go down to a desert road in Gaza where he made one convert, the Ethiopian eunuch (Acts 8:4–8, 26–40); when Peter was visited by an angel and told to have lunch at the home of the Roman centurion, Cornelius (Acts 10:1–33); and when, in hundreds of other localities, Christians sprang up as the news about the resurrected Christ and the Christian faith spread from person to person along the trade routes. In other words, there was no grand plan—simply a multitude of life-changing personal experiences.

Dr. Jun Escosar commented on the unexplained but undeniable transmission of the gospel throughout the world:

> There were almost no church buildings for the first 150 years. Meetings were conducted "from house to house" (Acts 5:42) and in small groups. There were no concise formulas or spiritual laws for salvation. The Christian faith was transmitted like the common cold, from person to person, as each tried to explain experiences of faith in his or her own way. Some learned about Christianity through friendships, stories of exorcisms or healing, or through the hired servants of Christians. People throughout the Roman Empire and beyond were converted and churches formed in every

way imaginable, and probably some ways that weren't. Without any precedents or strategic plan to follow, Christian missionaries were just ordinary people who were making it up as they went along. What held it all together was the common experience of the resurrected Christ.[2]

From Impromptu to Strategic Church Planting

In the years following the outpouring of the Holy Spirit at Pentecost, the spread of the gospel and the establishing of churches was unplanned. Christians simply walked through doors as they were opened for them. And in that way, the gospel spread like wildfire through dry brush.

Beginning with Paul's missionary journeys out of Antioch and with other apostles venturing out of Jerusalem, the spread of the gospel seemed to be far more planned and far less random. That didn't mean they simply followed the firmly set itinerary. At Troas, Paul and his team were forbidden by the Spirit of Jesus to preach the word in Bithynia, followed by a vision of a man saying, "'Come over to Macedonia and help us.' And when Paul had seen the vision, immediately we sought to go on into Macedonia, concluding that God had called us to preach the gospel to them" (Acts 16:9–10). So there was definitely an aspect of divine guidance in their missionary journeys.

That has been our experience in Victory and Every Nation. In the very early days of our movement, church planters were more likely to simply get a vision for a city and begin packing to go there. There was little emphasis on preparing for a church-planting venture. As a result, there were some weak starts and even failed attempts. In several regions, Every Nation now has a training and screening process for church planting candidates known as ABC3: **A**ssessment Center, Church-Planting **B**oot Camp, with ongoing **C**lusters for leadership, fellowship, and training, as well as ongoing **C**oaching and individual **C**onsulting.

At Victory, we discipled students and raised them up to be leaders, and as doors opened to pioneer new church plants in the provinces or opportunities arose to expand to different venues in Metro Manila, we would issue calls to these lay leaders to go into full-time ministry either as campus missionaries or pastors. We started our in-house leadership school to teach and train them in practical ministry and leadership skills. In the years succeeding that first decade, Victory has taken a much more strategic approach to church planting. We have an assessment process patterned after the Every Nation ABC3 church-planting initiative. Senior pastors of all our churches recommend candidates who have been fruitful in making disciples in small groups, display leadership capabilities, and have a sense of God's calling for vocational ministry. After assessment based on twelve criteria, the candidates undergo a three- or four-month training at our Every Nation Leadership Institute for campus ministry, church planting, or cross-cultural missions. They then continue to receive coaching as they serve in their ministry assignments.

Praying for Church Planting Initiatives

From our early experiences in ministry expansion through church planting, in the next two chapters, I offer a few suggestions on praying for church plants and those planting churches.

Pray for apostolic multiplication.

Fifth-generation churches are birthed by a parent church that planted another church, that planted another church, that planted another church, that planted another church. If you think of church planting in terms of children and grandchildren, Victory in Manila would then have 29 children, 60 grandchildren, 15 great-grandchildren, and 2 great-great-grandchildren—in all, 106 churches in the Philippines as of July 2021. Other Every Nation church-planting centers have also been extraordinarily productive in terms of multiplication, particularly King's Park International Church in Chapel Hill, North Carolina; Every Nation London; Grace Covenant Church in Chantilly, Virginia; churches birthed by teams sent out from Every Nation Dubai, UAE; numerous churches planted by the congregations of Every Nation in South Africa; and many others.

Our prayers should not focus on simply the birthing of a single church. That's not a recipe for changing a nation, let alone changing the world. I would not say that Every Nation leaders are dissatisfied with a successful church plant that does not produce other church plants, but the essential mission is to plant churches that will plant other churches that will plant other churches, and so on until the Lord's return. In short, we want to plant churches that will become apostolic church-planting centers. In the same way that changing the DNA of a child is impossible after his or her birth, changing the DNA of a church birthed without an apostolic vision for reproducing itself is highly unlikely. In Every Nation, we work to establish a church in a nation or region, and then, from that church, fill the nation with church plants that have the same apostolic DNA. Notwithstanding the insignificant beginnings, nothing that was so improbable has seemed so inevitable in retrospect as the expansion of our Every Nation churches throughout the world.

> ### CHURCH PLANTING PRAYERS
> *I pray for each church to be birthed with a sense of the apostolic mission to multiply and reproduce itself in new congregations throughout each region of the nation, beginning with the university campus communities.*

Pray for insight to break the missional code.

The action phrases of the Great Commission (Matthew 28:19) are: **go to every nation** and **make disciples**. "Every nation" is the easy part—easy in the sense that it is only a matter of deciding to "go." That is **certainly** a challenging idea, but not necessarily a complicated one. If all that we had to do was go, perhaps every nation would have already been Christianized. Complexity begins with what to do when one gets to a nation. In other words, how to "make disciples"—**in our context**, discovering the key to engaging, establishing, equipping, and empowering disciples (the 4Es). That is what is referred to as "**breaking** the missional code."

The best explanation of our discipleship strategy comes from Pastor Steve's book *WikiChurch*. With it, he also gives the following caution and a challenge to all pastors and church planters:

> I can understand why a leader would say, "Let's not try to reinvent the wheel. Let's find what is working and duplicate it in our church." However, a process works because it fits the culture you are trying to engage, the leadership team trying to implement it, and the people who are going to execute it.

> On numerous occasions, I have had people from the United States approach me to deliver their happy news—that they are doing small group discipleship in their church exactly the way we do it in the Philippines. Instead of the expected congratulations and a pat on the back, my typical response is, "Why in the world would you do that?" I will give them this explanation: "I'm in a city of twelve million people. Most of them live in poverty, very few young people have cars, it is an animistic Catholic culture, and the family structure is totally different from that in the West. The world you live in is completely different from Manila. Why would you copy us?"[3]

All missionaries and church planters, regardless of the cultural traditions of the target nation, have to develop their own system of effectively making disciples. They cannot simply download and install what we or others have developed through much prayer and experience.

CHURCH PLANTING PRAYERS

I pray for Holy Spirit-inspired wisdom to break the missional code by formulating a culturally appropriate process for engaging unbelievers for Christ with the gospel, for establishing biblical foundations in new believers from vastly different religious backgrounds and world-views, for equipping them to effectively minister to their friends, and for empowering them to reproduce themselves by making disciples.

Pray for next-generation leaders.

In chapter 4, I introduced the idea of thinking of the church as "the Lord's vineyard." While metaphors of sowing, reaping, and pruning are generally applied to individual spiritual growth, they can apply to the growth and expansion of the kingdom of God. One lesson we've learned from our experience at Victory is that constant pruning of our congregations enables new generations of leaders to emerge. It has never been the vision or strategy of Victory to become a single-location megachurch or even a network of satellite churches offering a video feed of the super-senior pastor. Victory church plants throughout Metro Manila, the Philippines, and Asia each have their own team of pastors, evangelists, and preachers. The benefit of developing new leaders has been very evident. In overgrown churches, there's nothing for upcoming leaders to do: no opportunities to serve, no challenges for growth, no pressing need to step forward to fill the role of leaders who have been sent out.

Our objective is to manage (and prune) church growth in a way that inspires, equips, and empowers those who are called to ministry. That doesn't mean we can simply create a system that forces people into career ministry roles; they have to be called by God and empowered with the appropriate spiritual gifts. That's where intercession and prayer for church-planting initiatives comes in. One of the most strategic prayers we can offer up to God is that by the power and influence of his Holy Spirit, he would send men and women who are called to be pastors, evangelists, missionaries, and church planters.

Pastor Rice tells a story of being invited by Pastor Steve and Allen Williams, a classmate, to a small campus meeting. Halfway through the leader's message on the baptism of the Holy Spirit, Rice jumped to his feet and said, "I've got to have what you're talking about!" The message abruptly ended, and the meeting never resumed. That night, Rice did receive the baptism of the Holy Spirit, which has changed the world. The part of the story that is seldom told is that a few of the leaders in the Starkville campus group had spent five days over the semester break, fasting and praying for God to send them future leaders to disciple. One of the first meetings after the period of prayer and fasting was when Rice walked into the meeting. After spending several nights at the ministry house, he showed up with his old pickup truck loaded and just moved in. It was a seminal event that set many things in motion. It was, in effect, the beginning of thousands of individual conversions on campus, scores of leaders going out, and many churches being planted all over the world.

CHURCH PLANTING PRAYERS

I pray for the Holy Spirit to send leaders to plant new churches. May they have the heart and calling to go into all the world, preach the gospel, and make disciples in every nation.

• • •

Everything we attempt to do should be undergirded with prayer—as individuals, as families, in business, and as a church. Can people get by in this world without a consistent prayer life? In many cases, it would seem to be so. However, the empowering presence of God is diminished, and only in the final analysis will it be revealed what one's life could have been—what fruit might have been produced, or what doors might have been opened to those in the habit of asking, seeking, and knocking.

Pray for apostolic multiplication.

I pray for each church to be birthed with a sense of the apostolic mission to multiply and reproduce itself in new congregations throughout each region of the nation, beginning with the university campus communities.

Pray for insight to break the missional code.

I pray for Holy Spirit-inspired wisdom to break the missional code by formulating a culturally appropriate process for engaging unbelievers for Christ with the gospel, for establishing biblical foundations in new believers from vastly different religious backgrounds and worldviews, for equipping them to effectively minister to their friends, and for empowering them to reproduce themselves by making disciples.

Pray for next-generation leaders.

I pray for the Holy Spirit to send leaders to plant new churches. May they have the heart and calling to go into all the world, preach the gospel, and make disciples in every nation.

CHAPTER SEVEN

VICTORY QUEZON CITY

In those days I, Daniel, was mourning for three weeks. I ate no delicacies, no meat or wine entered my mouth, nor did I anoint myself at all, for the full three weeks. . . . "The prince of the kingdom of Persia withstood me twenty-one days, but Michael, one of the chief princes, came to help me . . ."

—DANIEL 10:2-3, 13

In 1995, as Victory U-Belt, Makati, and Shangri-La were growing, the prospect of planting a church in Quezon City[1] energized my faith and significantly enlarged my vision. This was, after all, my community and where I had gone to school. Along with a team, I was being sent to plant a church with outreaches to the University of the Philippines (UP), Ateneo de Manila University, Miriam College, and Philippine Science High School. I realize Jesus had said, "A prophet has no honor in his own hometown" (John 4:44). I graduated twelve years earlier, in 1983, and though some of my professors were still there, the student body had turned over several times already. All the students were new to me, but the secular humanistic and intellectual elitist strongholds were the same.

Founded in 1908, UP has grown into a national university system with eight constituent universities in the Philippines. By one standard of measurement, it has become the premier university in the nation. Admission requirements are very high and acceptance rates very low. Of the almost 100,000 students who take the exam every year, approximately 11,000 are accepted—an admission rate of a little over 10 percent. It is especially difficult to get into the UP Diliman campus. Acceptance is primarily based on academic merit and not on the students' ability to pay tuition. There are many other quality educational institutions in the Philippines, both private and public, but if there were a single university system that churned out national leaders, it would be UP.

As of 2021, its alumni include seven Philippine presidents, fourteen Chief Justices of the Philippine Supreme Court, and the most members of the Philippine Senate and the House of Representatives. In addition to this, UP has produced dozens of National Scientists and National Artists, 15,000 doctors, 15,000 engineers, 8,000 lawyers, and 23,000 teachers. The Socialized Tuition System enacted by the Philippine Congress in 1988 created a tiered system of financial assistance, so being accepted in UP is far more difficult than the cost of tuition and fees. Though there is a strong sense of nationalism and willingness to serve the country as a national scholar (or what's known as *Iskolar ng Bayan*), being a student of the nation's top university has often become a source of pride and intellectual elitism.

• • •

While at UVA, I was exposed to the teachings of the Providence Foundation in the church pastored by Mark Beliles and Stephen McDowell. They instilled in me a vision for transforming a nation by discipling future leaders. Many of America's founding fathers reasoned from Scripture the principles of self- and institutional government, which are implied and at times stated explicitly in the Declaration of Independence and the first ten amendments of the US Constitution (the Bill of Rights). I believed those principles from the early American experiment in biblical self-government could find application in a Filipino context. That was the source of my initial dream to be involved in civil government, but I had responded to the calling to serve in full-time ministry. Just the idea of making disciples for Jesus Christ among the future leaders of our nation filled me with faith and hope for what our nation could become. It was the practical realization of

Pastor Steve's challenge: "Manny, if you're a senator, you're only one person. But if you're a pastor, you can disciple the senators, businessmen, government leaders, and everyone else." I saw that as a natural outcome of planting a church in Quezon City and reaching out to the students in UP Diliman.

• • •

During my summer internship in New York, I was given a prophetic word by the wife of one of the elders in the church I attended there. That was my first experience with a personal prophecy, and since it seemed a little mystical to me, I didn't think much about it. Even though she didn't know my background, she said that she saw me going on a long and winding road that eventually brought me back to where I had originally come from. She said I was on a stage addressing people. She didn't say I was preaching. It was just Jesus and me there on the platform. Nine years later, as we were starting the Victory congregation in Quezon City, walking and praying on the UP campus grounds, this prophetic word came rushing back to mind as a confirmation that God was truly with me in this endeavor. It was also the confirmation I would need, because nothing worked as any of us had anticipated. Nonetheless, in the Victory Quezon City initiative, we learned some valuable lessons about prayer, church planting, discipleship, and leadership development.

The Run-Up to Victory Quezon City

If you look at the map of Metro Manila, Quezon City doesn't appear to be that far away from Makati—only about fifteen kilometers. However, in terms of cultural distance and traffic congestion, it might as well have been in another province. Only a few of those on our pastoral team owned cars and could go there on short notice. A bus to UP Diliman took almost two hours each way. Even faced with these challenges, we had several students from UP Diliman and Ateneo de Manila University who had attended Victory Makati since 1987.

I was serving on the pastoral team of Victory Makati as well as the Sunday afternoon service at the Shangri-La Mall. Ferdie Cabiling was the youth pastor then. Joey Bonifacio, my partner in prayer, was still working as a bi-vocational businessman and pastor in Makati. We were one pastoral team serving two congregations. Pastor Steve was being stretched by the double duties and decided to designate one team member to be the lead pastor at Victory Makati. Not that we were casting lots for the assignment, as with the choosing of Matthias to replace Judas (Acts 1:21–26), but the lot did, in fact, fall to me.

. . .

In December of 1994, Jonathan Bocobo, who served as one of our pastors in Metro Manila and eventually short-term-missions director, was marrying his fiancée, Riza. The wedding venue happened to be in an auditorium along North Avenue in Quezon City. We were in the habit of evaluating every venue in terms of a potential outreach facility. It wasn't long before someone commented at the reception, "Hey, we should start a church here." There was no season of prayer or seeking God's direction, and no one was stepping up to punctuate the remark with a prophetic word. We were half-joking because it was a nice facility and starting a worship service was what we were all predisposed to do. But we soon realized the strategic significance of that location. The wedding venue was less than a kilometer from Philippine Science High School and only three kilometers from UP Diliman, both schools from which I had graduated. The joking quickly turned serious, and the "we should" became, "Manny, **you** should . . ."

Though our church-planting experience was quite limited in 1995, we had developed a simple strategy for establishing new congregations. We began by having meetings at available venues with Victory members from those areas. It was the one card we knew how to play and our go-to move—like a wildcard we could throw down in any situation. A plan quickly evolved, and before I knew it, I was being sent to Quezon City with the assumption that an afternoon service there would very quickly grow to have a few hundred students. Establishing a meeting near the UP Diliman campus was, to me, a thrilling proposition. In the back of my mind, however, I knew the objective was not just an afternoon meeting but to plant a self-sustaining congregation with an effective outreach to UP students.

Assuming the role of lead pastor in an established church was one thing; planting a church amid the intellectual strongholds of UP was something different altogether. While the former task required giftings that were already somewhat developed in my life—relational discipleship, biblical preaching, and pastoral leadership—becoming the lead pastor of a Victory church plant at UP was definitely out of my comfort zone. But there was no stopping it. Joey Bonifacio was set in as the lead pastor of Victory Makati, and within a week, I had mentally shifted gears from pastor to church planter.

Go Big or Go Home

Soon after we were sent out to start the new service in Quezon City, we discovered that the venue we wanted was unavailable for weekly meetings. In fact, there were no other facilities on or around the UP campus available for regular use. We pursued every option without a glimmer of success until our big vision just evaporated. We realized that Victory Quezon City and UP would require far more grit and determination than we had expected. Also, because my wife, Mini, and I had already uprooted ourselves from our current responsibilities, if the Victory Quezon City vision could not take off, we were uncertain about what we would do next.

• • •

The way we saw it, we were at an impasse with no available facilities to start meeting. Weary of our searching, Pastor Steve finally asked, "Why don't we just plant a church by starting small groups?" Actually, it was a rhetorical question, more a directive than an inquiry: "This is how we will birth Victory Quezon City. Begin with UP students in small groups on campus; they can still attend Sunday service in Victory Makati or Shangri-La, and when you get ten small groups of UP students established, we'll begin having a Sunday service for all Victory members from Quezon City." And with that, we had a plan.

Sounds simple, right? All we had to do was develop ten small groups of students from what was perhaps the most intellectually challenging student body in the Philippines. We had never tried to start a church in Metro Manila this way before, and though it's not an uncommon strategy now, it was a radical idea in 1995. You have to remember, we were experiencing a fast-growing harvest of new disciples in the wake of a genuine outpouring of the Holy Spirit. Concerning our strategy, we were simply making it up as we went.

We have had discipleship groups from the inception of Victory. However, basic training classes on discipleship are different from ongoing small groups. The question was: What were we to do with church members after they finished basic discipleship training? From 1993 to 1994, our discipleship groups were like mini church services. Six to eight people would gather to watch one person teach. There wasn't much interaction or sharing of lives. We were still working through our philosophy of ministry and had yet to figure out what we needed to accomplish and how to organize it in the church. We studied what others were doing, went on a fact-finding trip, and did a lot of prayer and fasting. After several false starts, attempting to incorporate small groups into the life of the church, we decided to start on the fringes with the new people, tweak the approach, make it work, and then begin incorporating it into the congregation. The transition for us was that our Victory small groups would no longer be leader-centered; rather, they would be member-centered. Small group leaders helped facilitate interaction through Bible study—in other words, sharing their lives with one another, not teaching them. In our worship services, we had the opportunity to praise God with all our hearts and experience the renewing presence of the Holy Spirit. There the word of God was proclaimed with great boldness and conviction. In our small groups, we were free to share our hopes and fears, victories and setbacks, as we learned to apply God's word in our daily lives. The most important component, especially for new people who had not yet come to faith in Christ, was that our small groups became a place for carrying one another's burdens through prayer.

$$\cdot \quad \cdot \quad \cdot$$

I take comfort in several things that I learned from Pastor Steve and which I could identify with in planting Victory Quezon City.

First, though Pastor Steve responds to any opportunity to preach the gospel, he didn't see himself as a gifted evangelist like Rice Broocks, Ferdie Cabiling, Jun Escosar, or others. Neither did I.

Second, Pastor Steve was a newlywed when he first came to Manila in 1984. So was I when we started Victory Quezon City. We had each been married less than a year when we became unexpected or accidental church planters. That didn't stop Steve and Deborah, and Mini and I followed right along. I found out later that most church-planting consultants encouraged newly married couples to give it a few years before launching a church-planting initiative. The experience of being baptized in the Holy Spirit doesn't automatically solve all marital conflicts, but learning to depend on his empowering presence enabled Mini and I to have unity of mind and purpose instead of dwelling on each other's flaws. My wife had been discipled well as a college student and knew how to reproduce strong followers of Christ. I appreciated her being in full agreement and faith for our new venture.

Third, Pastor Steve was a man of prayer and believed in the importance of corporate prayer in the early life of the church. Since we were pioneering a new church, this became our strategy as well.

With the objective clearly laid out before us, Mini and I, along with Neil Bernardino, Edgar Gorre, and a few women leaders, began small group meetings with UP students who were already Victory members from Makati and Shangri-La. We started in January 1995 with two small groups. We were a motley crew that could only meet outdoors. What we did more than anything else was pray. We prayed on the UP campus; we prayer-walked around the campus; we engaged in spiritual warfare against the strongholds of intellectual pride and secular humanism; we interceded for students, professors, and university administrators. We prayed for six months and added only a few students. My convictions about the importance of prayer to guide, provide, and empower everything we attempted had grown deeper over time. Now we were in a season that tested our faith in the effectiveness of prayer.

Having prepared the soil for planting, we began to reach out to students in July 1995 with a team of short-term missionaries from southern California led by Gregg Tipton. Gregg preached the gospel at the Alumni Center after presenting the Hell's Bells seminar for two successive nights. The results were more than promising, with approximately forty students responding to the message. We then got busy discipling these new believers. By the end of that semester, we had our ten small groups of UP students, and Victory members from Makati and Shangri-La began attending the Sunday morning service at a mini-mall located on the perimeter of the university grounds. By the end of the year, almost 150 people were part of Victory Quezon City. Soon after the next school year started in 1996, we had another outreach on campus with Steve Hollander and made dozens of new disciples as well.

In 1997, Pastor Rice Broocks came to UP for a two-day outreach, and approximately 300 students made the decision to surrender their lives to Jesus Christ. The receptivity to the gospel was remarkable. Seeing that many students openly wanting to follow Christ was one of the most glorious moments of my life.

I personally led the prayer meetings for the first three to four years of the church, from when there were only about a dozen of us in 1995. Many of those early prayer meetings were held beside Villamor Hall, UP's 2,000-seat performing arts theater. Our little group prayed, confessed our faith, and prophesied that one day we would fill that auditorium. In the tenth year, we did meet in Villamor Hall with almost 1,500 members of our church. At Victory Quezon City's fifteenth anniversary in 2010, there was an Every Nation world conference in Manila. During one of the conference sessions, we asked who had been saved in the initial campus outreaches in the first few years. Over 100 rose to their feet.

Fasting and Praying for Church Plants

Successfully birthing a church in the realm of the Spirit comes before successfully birthing it in the natural. The apostle Paul wrote to the church that he planted in Thessalonica, "Finally, brothers, pray for us, that the word of the Lord may speed ahead and be honored, as happened among you" (2 Thessalonians 3:1). Here are a few prayer points for church plants and for those sent out to do the planting.

Pray for God's perfect timing.

The church-planting team should neither be anxious to get ahead of nor lag behind what God has destined them to do. Instead, they are to sense God's timing. This is reminiscent of Moses' conversation with God in Exodus 33:14–16:

> **And he said,** "My presence will go with you, and I will give you rest." And he said to him, "If your presence will not go with me, do not bring us up from here. For how shall it be known that I have found favor in your sight, I and your people? Is it not in your going with us . . . ?"

The two operating ideas in this passage are waiting on the Lord for his timing and the necessity of the empowering presence of the Holy Spirit. We should neither be over-anxious nor over-careful about the timing to launch—not presumptuous about our success or fearful about potential failure. Through our many church-planting initiatives, we've learned to step out in faith at the Spirit's leading and, at the same time, realize that we are totally dependent on God's power and provision. Starting a new meeting or planting a new church had, up to that point, been an easy thing to do. We assumed that an afternoon service in UP would very quickly grow to a few hundred. However, when all the doors seemed closed, we had to adjust our understanding of God's timing. In retrospect, the Holy Spirit seemed to be saying that we needed to spend six months of consistent prayer and fasting to prepare the way for gospel proclamation.

CHURCH PLANTING PRAYERS

I pray that your Holy Spirit would confirm our plans to plant churches; confirm the times and seasons of planting and harvesting; give grace to the team and an awareness of your empowering presence. May we wait on you in prayer and obey with boldness.

Pray for God's wisdom.

We had been close to abandoning the idea of planting a church in Quezon City when Pastor Steve suggested, "Why don't we start with small groups?" Since we'd never started a church that way, we had failed to even consider that approach. However, we had taken the suggestion as the Holy Spirit's direction. Deciding to begin a regular church service for the community when we had ten functioning small groups of student disciples caused us to focus on discipleship and winning students for Christ. In many parts of the world, particularly North America and the Philippines, it's not that difficult to launch a church with a collection of Christians from other churches. We had discovered that with Victory Shangri-La. Launching with a considerable percentage of new believers is harder because it requires church planters to engage culture and community with the gospel. Starting with new believers from the campus is even more challenging. Pastor Rice's admonition to visitors from other church groups during the initial U-Belt outreach was ringing in our minds. We plant churches to reach the lost, not the already churched. In retrospect, we are grateful for God's wisdom for us to establish a church with one foot on campus and another in the community.

CHURCH PLANTING PRAYERS

Lord, enable me to remain faithful to my calling—to honor you by establishing Christ-centered, Spirit-empowered, socially responsible churches and campus ministries in every nation. Send out missionaries and church planters to both students and people from the community, who have been prepared by your Holy Spirit to accept the gift of salvation by grace through faith and to follow you fully as disciples and leaders.

Pray for God to move the immovable, to open doors that no man can shut.

There are occasions when the timing of a church plant can be delayed, particularly when there are well-entrenched spiritual strongholds. One example was when an angel appeared to Daniel in a vision as he was fasting and praying for understanding.

> *In those days I, Daniel, was mourning for three weeks. I ate no delicacies, no meat or wine entered my mouth, nor did I anoint myself at all, for the full three weeks.... "The prince of the kingdom of Persia withstood me twenty-one days, but Michael, one of the chief princes, came to help me ..."*
> —DANIEL 10:2–3, 13

This is a glimpse into the world the apostle Paul referred to as wrestling "against the rulers, against the authorities, against the cosmic powers over this present darkness, against the spiritual forces of evil in the heavenly places" (Ephesians 6:12). There is far more to understand about this realm and the impact of our prayers than we can ever know on this side of eternity. This is simply one example of answered prayers and open doors that were the result of a victory in spiritual warfare. I'm not suggesting our focus and length of time devoted to prayer is the formula for every church plant. The reasons for the relatively long period of concentrated prayer and fasting for our church plant in Quezon City are beyond our understanding. Perhaps the stronghold of intellectual elitism had something to do with the approach we ended up taking.

CHURCH PLANTING PRAYERS

In the mighty and powerful name of Jesus of Nazareth, I bind the powers of darkness that oppose the advancement of the kingdom of God in this campus, this city, and this country. I pray for open eyes and open hearts for those who have been called and destined for eternal salvation.

Pray for the Holy Spirit to assemble the right team.

There are a lot of moving parts that go into a successful church-planting initiative. In addition to undergirding the effort with intercessory prayer and fasting for the souls of new disciples, there are issues of funding, housing, facilities, on-campus permissions, assembling the launch team, and pre-launch preparations—just to name a few. All of this can take a great deal of time and effort. Some church planters are more gifted organizationally than others, and a leader overwhelmed with administrative challenges will have additional difficulties. Sometimes a deficiency in the gift of administration, the ability to delegate, or the gifts and talents of the launch-team members can make it hard for the fledgling church plant to be firmly established. Consequently, the struggle can go on for years.

We would not have been nearly as successful without my wife, Mini, who discipled new believers and set up our kids' church; Neil and Blanche Bernardino who served as a campus missionary and finance officer, respectively; and Edgar and Jeng Gorre, who taught and raised up leaders. Winston and Gigi Reyes were eventually sent out from Victory Quezon City to begin another church plant. With my background in business from UVA, I had a good grasp of administration, but more than that was my commitment to prayer. I saw those functions as the roles I was to play. Eventually, the first batch of students in our church graduated from the university, and several sensed the call of God to go into vocational ministry. One by one, Sharon Milan-Mayo, Carlos Antonio, Raya Bambico-Llanto, Christian Flores, Erwin Ramos, and others joined our campus and administrative staff a few years after they graduated. We had an extraordinary team.

As Jim Collins wrote in his best-selling classic, *Good to Great,* one of the five things that separates merely good companies from those that are truly great is "getting the right people on the bus." Few church-planting teams start with all the giftings they need. But if they wait for a fully functioning team, they could be waiting forever. They go with the understanding that they will have to quickly raise up leaders with those other giftings.

CHURCH PLANTING PRAYERS

Lord, you alone know the needs of the church plant and those whom you have called and predestined to be a part of this work. Send us campus missionaries, worship leaders, and administrators, as well as those with the capacity and heart for generous giving.

Pray for church planters' relationships.

Starting a new church can put a lot of pressure on relationships. That's why experienced leaders assessing the readiness of church-planting teams encourage newlyweds to give their relationship time to settle on a solid foundation before planting a church. Mini and I had been married less than a year at the beginning of the outreach to UP. What made the difference for us was the great team that went with us and the support from our friends across town at Victory Makati. There are Every Nation missionaries and church planters continually going into all the world to make disciples. In many cases, they are going into very isolated situations or creative-access nations where spiritual forces of darkness oppose everything they try to do and every aspect of their lives.

CHURCH PLANTING PRAYERS

I pray for every married couple and every team member. Guard their hearts and minds from the influences, attacks, and schemes of the enemy. Fill each one of them with the Holy Spirit, with boldness, and with discernment. Empower them for victory in the spiritual battles they will inevitably be engaged in.

Pray for God's favor concerning the right facility at the right time.

With regard to praying and fasting for places to meet, two landmark stories come to mind.

We have an Every Nation church in one of the most radical and repressive anti-Christian nations (also one of the poorest). There are fewer Christians there than in any nation on the planet. A few years ago, an Every Nation leader serving in that nation was sentenced to many years in prison for preaching the gospel. How God delivered him after just two years is a miraculous story, but it didn't end there. The powers-that-be decided to sell off some state property. Even though there is fierce opposition to the gospel in that nation, it was discovered that if a church owns the property, constitutionally, it can hold as many services as it wants. This small, impoverished body of believers in an extremely poor nation raised a third of the funds for the purchase. Every Nation churches in Asia supplied another one-third and the final one-third came from American partners. The church purchased the property, located less than a kilometer from the largest private university in the nation.

In 2020 just before the coronavirus pandemic halted much movement in the world, we were in the process of purchasing land in the University Belt in Manila. Because the facility is located at ground zero of our primary mission field, where we had been preaching the gospel and making disciples since 1984, we had asked God for property there for many years. We trusted God that this would be our inheritance for generations to come, along with land in Quezon City and Malate, two other university hubs in Metro Manila.

By faith and God's miraculous provision, in 2018 we had purchased property on Katipunan Avenue in Quezon City. Now, by another miracle, we had money for half a piece of land that was up for purchase in the U-Belt. Land there is not easy to come by, as every square meter is used and maximized. We knew it was providential that we found property that was for sale and the owner was willing to sell us half.

In the course of negotiations, we were given a lower price, but that meant not paying full taxes. We decided not to entertain such an option, but doing this meant those selling the land would agree to receive less than what they were asking for. They were, at first, not amenable to the amount. Even after many discussions, recomputations, and prayers, we had hit a wall and didn't know what to do next. We met to pray and fast, knowing we had to trust God and make one final appeal. Jun Escosar recalls:

> We wanted to purchase the property but also had to be upfront about how we would go about this. Even if what we wanted to do meant our paying more and the owners' receiving less, we knew it was the right thing to do. At the end of our day of prayer and fasting, someone suggested that Dr. Nixon Ng and I meet the owners and ask them to agree. Talk about God using the foolish things of the world to confound the wise! We made a bold pitch for what we could only afford by a miracle—and they had already given us a definite **no**. That day, unexpectedly and inexplicably, the owners agreed to our terms and accepted our offer.

The Psalmist wrote, "For you bless the righteous, O LORD; you cover him with favor as with a shield" (Psalm 5:12). There have been countless examples of God's provision with regard to church facilities. Over and over, we have seen that "The king's heart is a stream of water in the hand of the LORD; he turns it wherever he will" (Proverbs 21:1). We do not completely see or understand the harvest the Lord will bring in these places—whether it's in a radical and repressive anti-Christian nation or the heart of Manila's University Belt. But we do know that God in his providence and sovereignty guides us into his plans for us and gives us favor, provision, and wisdom.

> **CHURCH PLANTING PRAYERS**
>
> *I pray for favor and provision to secure facilities in the most strategic locations—at the crossroads of campus and community—where the church can effectively engage people with the gospel, make disciples, and train leaders.*

• • •

Planting a church in Quezon City in 1995 was an extraordinary learning experience in the power of prayer to birth a church at the epicenter of one of the nation's most significant strongholds. Nothing happened according to plan, and the impact of our experience changed the way we planted churches from that point. In 2007, as I was asked to take on a different role overseeing our churches in the Philippines, we transitioned the leadership of the Quezon City congregation to Edgar and Jeng Gorre. Given the church-planting experience in Quezon City, my estimation of the power and necessity of prayer only intensified.

Thereafter, I invited several intercessors from across Victory in Metro Manila to a weekly corporate prayer meeting in the Every Nation Building to pray for our church movement, the nation, and the world. This prayer gathering has been going on for over fifteen years now. We normally have twenty to thirty intercessors in attendance. When the students of the Every Nation Leadership Institute Schools of Ministry are there, it swells to about eighty to a hundred people. Years later, when we constructed phase 2 of the Every Nation Building, we added a prayer chapel for the exclusive purpose of prayer.

Pray for God's perfect timing.

I pray that your Holy Spirit would confirm our plans to plant churches; confirm the times and seasons of planting and harvesting; give grace to the team and an awareness of your empowering presence. May we wait on you in prayer and obey with boldness.

Pray for God's wisdom.

Lord, enable me to remain faithful to my calling—to honor you by establishing Christ-centered, Spirit-empowered, socially responsible churches and campus ministries in every nation. Send out missionaries and church planters to both students and people from the community, who have been prepared by your Holy Spirit to accept the gift of salvation by grace through faith and to follow you fully as disciples and leaders.

Pray for God to move the immovable, to open doors that no man can shut.

In the mighty and powerful name of Jesus of Nazareth, I bind the powers of darkness that oppose the advancement of the kingdom of God in this campus, this city, and this country. I pray for open eyes and open hearts for those who have been called and destined for eternal salvation.

Pray for the Holy Spirit to assemble the right team.

Lord, you alone know the needs of the church plant and those whom you have called and predestined to be a part of this work. Send us campus missionaries, worship leaders, and administrators, as well as those with the capacity and heart for generous giving.

Pray for church planters' relationships.

I pray for every married couple and every team member. Guard their hearts and minds from the influences, attacks, and schemes of the enemy. Fill each one of them with the Holy Spirit, with boldness, and with discernment. Empower them for victory in the spiritual battles they will inevitably be engaged in.

Pray for God's favor concerning the right facility at the right time.

I pray for favor and provision to secure facilities in the most strategic locations—at the crossroads of campus and community—where the church can effectively engage people with the gospel, make disciples, and train leaders.

CHAPTER EIGHT

THE ROLE OF
THE SPIRIT IN PRAYER

. . . the Spirit intercedes for the saints according to the will of God.
—ROMANS 8:27

The apostles and the early church understood the outpouring of the Holy Spirit in terms of the restoration of the personal presence of God. Of course, that is not to suggest that the Spirit was ever absent in the world. For the eternal and omnipresent God who fills all creation, there is no place that is not here and no time that is not now. That being said, the Spirit of God whose manifest presence was occasional under the Old Covenant was now poured out upon all believers. In the New Covenant, "no longer shall each one teach his neighbor and each his brother, saying, 'Know the LORD,' for they shall all know me, from the least of them to the greatest" (Jeremiah 31:34). It was also the promise of God through Ezekiel: "I will put my Spirit within you, and cause you to walk in my statutes" (Ezekiel 36:27). And it was the fulfillment of the prophecy of Joel about the outpouring of the Spirit on all flesh (Joel 2:28–29).

On the day of Pentecost when the believers were gathered in one place, they were all filled with the Holy Spirit and began to speak in tongues. Eventually, the apostle Peter stood to explain:

"But this is what was uttered through the prophet Joel: 'And in the last days it shall be, God declares, that I will pour out my Spirit on

all flesh, and your sons and your daughters shall prophesy, and your young men shall see visions, and your old men shall dream dreams; even on my male servants and female servants in those days I will pour out my Spirit, and they shall prophesy.'"

—ACTS 2:16–18

The outpouring of the Holy Spirit was essential to how the early believers understood their present life as inheritors of the promise and citizens of the kingdom of God. They were no longer to be known only as a people who were radically adherent to the Law, but the people of the Resurrection and the empowering Holy Spirit.

• • •

I was first exposed to the teachings of Professor Gordon D. Fee during my studies at Asbury Theological Seminary. He did not come to Asbury while I was a student there, but I read his books and listened to many of his lectures online. He is not only a renowned New Testament professor; he is almost without peer as a Pentecostal theologian and commentator on the Holy Spirit in the church and in the lives of believers. In his exhaustive 914-page commentary, *God's Empowering Presence: The Holy Spirit in the Letters of Paul,* Dr. Fee demonstrates that the Holy Spirit's empowering presence is central to Paul's experience and theology.

The traditional view, fostered by the reformers and perpetuated by generations of Protestants, is that "justification by faith" was the primary (if not the exclusive) key to Paul's understanding of the person and work of Jesus Christ. In many evangelical and Protestant circles, Christ's sacrifice is understood as the means to pay the immeasurable debt and to redeem the souls of mankind. It is appropriated by the believer, not by good works; it is by grace through faith alone. That is absolutely true and is, in part, the foundational rock of Christianity. It is, however, not the fullness of understanding of what God has done for us in Christ. That sacrifice, the payment for our redemption, is ultimately realized by Jesus' promise to give us the gift of the Holy Spirit. The presence and power of the indwelling Spirit is the confirmation that the believer has truly been justified by faith and empowered for service in God's kingdom. This is affirmed by the following Scriptures:

"If you love me, you will keep my commandments. And I will ask the Father, and he will give you another Helper, to be with you forever, even the Spirit of truth, whom the world cannot receive, because it neither sees him nor knows him. You know him, for he dwells with you and will be in you."

—JOHN 14:15–17

And Peter said to them, "Repent and be baptized every one of you in the name of Jesus Christ for the forgiveness of your sins, and you will receive the gift of the Holy Spirit."

—ACTS 2:38

"And I remembered the word of the Lord, how he said, 'John baptized with water, but you will be baptized with the Holy Spirit.' If then God gave the same gift to them as he gave to us when we believed in the Lord Jesus Christ, who was I that I could stand in God's way?"

—ACTS 11:16–17

In his epistle to the Romans, the letter known for his explanation of the righteousness that is imputed to us by grace through faith, the apostle Paul wrote about walking in the Spirit, praying in the Spirit, the witness of the Spirit, serving with the Spirit, the leading of the Spirit, the mind set on the Spirit, the law of the Spirit, the gifts of the Spirit, and the demonstration of the Spirit. As much as Paul's theology was about our legal justification, it was equally centered on the empowering presence of the Holy Spirit.

Prayer Empowered by the Holy Spirit

Nowhere in his epistle to the Roman church does the apostle Paul more directly address Spirit-empowered prayer than in Romans 8:26–27:

Likewise the Spirit helps us in our weakness. For we do not know what to pray for as we ought, but the Spirit himself intercedes for us with groanings too deep for words. And he who searches hearts knows what is the mind of the Spirit, because the Spirit intercedes for the saints according to the will of God.

In those fifty-nine words, as in many other short passages from Romans, there are countless insights and applications to unpack. We will look at four here.

Paul's focus seems to be on individual believers and their lack of understanding of God's will.

The application seems to be more personal than corporate. "Our weakness" is that in the midst of difficult or confusing situations, believers "do not know **what to pray for as they ought**." The New American Standard Bible translates it as, "We do not know what to pray for as we should."

Most church historians believe Paul wrote the epistle to the Romans around AD 57 under the reign of the emperor Nero. Nero's predecessor, the emperor Claudius, had ordered all the Jews to leave Rome in the early AD 50s. Paul had not yet been to Rome but had heard firsthand accounts from Aquila and Priscilla, who had fled Rome and joined him in Corinth (Acts 18:1–3). The remaining Christians in the Roman congregation were persecuted for their refusal to worship the emperor or take part in sacrifices to gods, as was expected of those living in the Roman Empire. So, at the time of Paul's writing, there was growing persecution and a sense of terrible things that were about to come upon the church.

At the same time, there was a prominent idea that martyrdom was an honor. In other words, what the first leaders of the church in Jerusalem faced was also becoming the fate of thousands of Roman Christians. Only a few verses earlier, Paul wrote:

> *The Spirit himself bears witness with our spirit that we are children of God, and if children, then heirs—heirs of God and fellow heirs with Christ, provided we suffer with him in order that we may also be glorified with him. For I consider that the sufferings of this present time are not worth comparing with the glory that is to be revealed to us.*
>
> **—ROMANS 8:16–18**

Then in AD 64, Rome burned. The fires, lasting six days, destroyed 75 percent of the city. It was generally considered that Nero himself ordered the fires to be lit for his own amusement, and the Christians were conveniently blamed. What followed was a systematic persecution of Christians. In his book *Annals*, the Roman historian Tacitus wrote about the events a few years after: "In their very deaths they were made the subjects of sport: for they were covered with the hides of wild beasts, and worried to death by dogs, or nailed to crosses, or set fire to, and when the day waned, burned to serve for the evening lights." The emperors Claudius, Nero, and Nero's successor, Domitian, were despicable characters, each in their own time attempting to outdo the brutality of their predecessor against the church.

Can you see the conflict the Roman believers would encounter in the near future? Should they pray with all their hearts to be delivered or accept what seemed to be the inevitable honor of martyrdom? Not an easy decision, and far more intense than many of us will ever face. More commonly, our prayers are for things we desire to have or do. There's nothing wrong with that. To the church in Philippi, Paul wrote, "Do not be anxious about anything, but in everything by prayer and supplication with thanksgiving let your requests be made known to God" (Philippians 4:6). Or as a modern translation says, "Don't worry about anything, but pray about everything" (CEV). Even in those situations that are less threatening than martyrdom in the arena, the question plagues many dedicated disciples: Am I truly seeking God's will, or am I seeking my own will? In many cases, it's not a matter of unsurrendered areas in one's life. We desire to do God's will; the difficulty is figuring out what that is and finding the courage to follow. To that person making a career choice or to the one facing martyrdom, Paul writes, "For we do not know what to pray for as we ought . . . And he who searches hearts knows what is the mind of the Spirit, because the Spirit intercedes for the saints according to the will of God" (Roman 8:26–27).

SPIRIT-LED PRAYER AND FASTING

Father, I ask that your Holy Spirit would show me how to pray in accordance with your perfect will for <insert friend or family member's name>. Empower me to pray in the Spirit and give me your assurance that you will answer our prayers according to your will. I ask for your sovereign grace to soften our hearts to surrender unconditionally to your plan. In time open our eyes to see, understand, and accept your will.

The Holy Spirit desires for you to be an instrument of intercession for others.

When Christians begin to put limitations on what the Spirit can do or prescriptions for what he must automatically do, we are making the mistake the Scripture warns us against: "Do not quench the Spirit. Do not despise prophecies, but test everything; hold fast what is good" (1 Thessalonians 5:19–21). Even though in Romans 8:26–27 Paul focuses on the Spirit helping us with our weaknesses regarding prayer for our own needs, to limit the need for Spirit-led prayer to personal application only does, in fact, quench or limit what the Spirit desires to accomplish through our prayers. The Spirit desires to inspire you, empower you, and use you to pray for other people, churches, leaders, and nations. When things are going well for us (no crisis, no conflict, no confusion about God's will), does that excuse us from fasting, prayer, and intercession for others? No, not in the least. Paul says we are members of one body and we are to carry one another's burdens. If our only prayer concerns were for our own problems, it would be contrary to everything we know about the kingdom of God. God wants each of us to be acutely sensitive to the Spirit as he leads us to intercede for people who we know need his grace, power, and protection. In addition, he wants us to be sensitive to his impressions to pray for those in circumstances about which we have no knowledge.

Pastor Jim Laffoon has a unique prophetic gifting that he consistently applies to intercessory prayer. Those gifts operate through him in ways that are quite extraordinary. "As Christians, we are exhorted to watch and pray," he says. "Most Christians pray, but far fewer of them watch. Consequently, they tend to pray reactively (after Satan has already attacked) rather than allowing the Spirit to lead us to pray proactively." A few years ago, we invited Pastor Jim to come to Manila and teach on proactive prayer to several hundred Victory intercessors. In those sessions, he talked about being an intercessory watchman—one of the primary passages coming from the book of Ezekiel: "Son of man, I have made you a watchman for the house of Israel. Whenever you hear a word from my mouth, you shall give them warning from me" (Ezekiel 3:17). There were numerous instances in which Jim and other members of the team were prompted by the Holy Spirit to pray proactively for unknown needs. There were, of course, many similarly inspired prayers that continue to be a mystery. Only God knows what did or did not happen. Pastor Jim commented, "There are a number of people who I feel called to serve as a watchman. Some of them don't even know that's what I do. Many times, I just sit before the Lord with the question in my mind, *Lord, is there anything you want me to know; anything I should pray about on their behalf?*"

· · ·

One remarkable example of this kind of proactive prayer comes from Dr. Jun Escosar, as told in his book. In May 2015, three Every Nation missionaries from Malaysia were leading an Every Nation Campus retreat with about 120 Chinese students in one of the major cities in China.

There was a break on the afternoon of the second day before the closing session. Students were on the beach chatting, sharing life, and playing games. Around 5:30 p.m. they saw a van and a police car speed into the hotel compound. Policemen came pouring out of the van. Immediately, they rounded up everyone on the beach and corralled them into the hotel. They were incredibly swift, and all this happened in just a few minutes. The police began collecting the computers, every piece of printed material, and the names of everyone present.

As soon as our national leaders realized that it was a raid, they instructed the non-Chinese members of our Every Nation team to leave the area. Those three, Jacob and two other Malaysians, began walking away from the hotel. The police officers were shouting at everybody and detaining anyone trying to escape, including six other tourists only a few steps away from the three.

The miracle was that while they were walking away, somehow, the police did not see them. In Jacob's mind, he kept asking, *How could the police not see us when they saw six other tourists right in front of us?* It was as if the Lord had placed an invisible covering over them so that they were able to walk right past the police without being noticed. They kept walking without looking back—down the stairway, away from the hotel, toward the beach. They hid behind a big rock along the shore about 300 meters away from the hotel until almost midnight, interceding for the rest of the church members that were being interrogated.

There's another side to this story. Phuah Boon Leong, a teacher by profession, is a faithful member of our Every Nation church in Kuala Lumpur. Phuah and his wife are intercessors and lead the prayer ministry of the church. While the Every Nation Campus retreat was ongoing in China, Phuah, who was in Kuala Lumpur, had a vision that led him to pray earnestly for Jacob and his team. In Phuah's words: "I remember seeing a beach scene where people were running helter-skelter due to the presence of police. Some stood still, but Jacob and two others were hiding behind a rock and there was water around their feet. I remember being jolted out of this vision and praying for safety and the covering of God to be upon these faithful men. I prayed that the authorities would not see them and that no one would suffer any harassment during the search."[1]

SPIRIT-LED PRAYER AND FASTING

God, I do not know how to pray as I should; but you know every aspect of all things that concern us. Speak to my spirit, impress upon my mind what you want me to intercede for. I hold up <insert friend or family member's name> with my prayers, even as Aaron and Hur held up the arms of Moses until Israel prevailed (Exodus 17:12).

The Holy Spirit inspires and empowers us to pray effectively for things beyond our understanding.

Paul described a similar occurrence in a letter to the Corinthian church: "For if I pray in a tongue, my spirit prays but my mind is unfruitful. What am I to do? I will pray with my spirit, but I will pray with my mind also; I will sing praise with my spirit, but I will sing with my mind also" (1 Corinthians 14:14–15). Paul's letters to the Romans and Corinthians were written to different congregations in different countries under different circumstances, which suggests that Spirit-led intercession beyond our understanding was a frequent experience in the life of the apostle Paul.

One contemporary example was how the leaders of Every Nation London were led to plant a church in China. Wolfi Eckleben, senior pastor of the church in London, explains: "Many years ago, in a prayer meeting for the nations, there was a word in tongues which was repeated over and over. We discerned that it meant something, and discovered later that it was the name of a city in central China."

This is one of the most visited cities in China and the location of the Nestorian Stele, a stone monument erected around AD 781 that chronicled 150 years of Christianity in China. Taizong, the reigning monarch, welcomed the Christian missionary Alopen in AD 635 and arranged for the translation of the biblical writings he had brought with him for the Imperial Library. Three years later Taizong built the first Christian church in China and recognized twenty-one priests. Alopen became the bishop over the many churches established throughout China. As a result of persecution, the Christian church disappeared from recorded history in the early tenth century, but was reintroduced by the Mongols. When the Nestorian Stele was discovered in the seventeenth century, the Chinese were surprised to find that the "new" religion being preached by the missionaries had actually been in existence in China for more than ten centuries.

Wolfi recounts: "As a leadership team, we concluded that the Lord was leading us to go on a mission there, and that resulted in seven years of work in missions, with about 150 individuals responding to the call to go to China from London. We went to the campus in that city each year to engage, establish, and equip disciples, and then empowered local leaders to start a church. Every Nation now has a thriving church in that city, led by a couple that was reached on one of our mission trips there."

SPIRIT-LED PRAYER AND FASTING

Lord, I will pray in the Spirit and with my understanding that the thing I do not even know to ask might be accomplished in your perfect time and place.

The Spirit himself intercedes for us with groanings too deep for words (Romans 8:26).

Too often, contemporary readers picture Jesus as a stoic philosopher and teacher, living above the raw emotions of everyday life. However, the real Jesus rejoiced when good things happened, celebrated at weddings, raged at the hypocrisy of religious leaders, and used a whip to drive money changers out of the temple. In my mind, I can see him dancing, laughing, telling jokes. We know, of course, no one could tell a story like Jesus. But he also grieved, cried, and groaned over lost loved ones, as was the case with the death and burial of Lazarus. "When Jesus therefore saw her weeping, and the Jews also weeping which came with her, he groaned in the spirit, and was troubled" (John 11:33, KJV), and a few verses later, "Jesus therefore again groaning in himself cometh to the grave" (John 11:38, KJV).

Paul continued with another aspect of Spirit-empowered prayer. "Likewise the Spirit helps us in our weakness. For we do not know what to pray for as we ought, but the Spirit himself intercedes for us with groanings too deep for words" (Romans 8:26). "Likewise" indicates this is similar to something else mentioned before. Paul was referring back to verses 22–23:

> For we know that the whole creation has been **groaning** together in the pains of childbirth until now. And not only the creation, but we ourselves, who have the firstfruits of the Spirit, **groan inwardly** as we wait eagerly for adoption as sons, the redemption of our bodies.

Because we have been filled with the Holy Spirit (the firstfruits of the promise), we now groan within ourselves for the full manifestation of that promise. I'm not suggesting that we need a movement of public groaning. The groaning Paul refers to was within one's self. Public groaning is a little too reminiscent of religious leaders who were in the habit of displaying their holiness with long dramatic appeals to heaven (Matthew 6:5). Nevertheless, in many places throughout the Scriptures, travailing in prayer is analogous to the pains of childbirth. Applied in a spiritual sense, it is symbolic of birthing unseen realities by prayer and fasting.

Jesus compared the coming kingdom of God to a woman giving birth. "Whenever a woman is in labor she has pain, because her hour has come; but when she gives birth to the child, she no longer remembers the anguish because of the joy that a child has been born into the world" (John 16:21, NASB). That was not surprising because the prophet Isaiah had used that imagery before—that is, labor pains that immediately precede a new birth (Isaiah 21:3–4; 66:7–9).

The apostle Paul uses the same imagery in his letter to the Galatian church: ". . . my little children, for whom I am again in the anguish of childbirth until Christ is formed in you!" (Galatians 4:19). The context and Paul's repeated use of the child-birthing imagery leads one to believe that, to the apostle, it was more than a literary metaphor—it was an actual experience of intercessory prayer.

Isaiah refers to this travailing as well: "Out of the anguish of his soul he shall see and be satisfied; by his knowledge shall the righteous one, my servant, make many to be accounted righteous, and he shall bear their iniquities" (Isaiah 53:11).

I have heard of people travailing in prayer (i.e., with groaning too deep for words) as one laboring, until they receive the assurance that their prayers have been heard. As a result, they have peace that surpasses all understanding about the matter. I have also heard stories about intercessors who identified with (or took on) the grief, pain, or separation of those for whom they prayed. The apostle Paul is talking about a prayer that cannot just be expressed in words. It is so deep and far beyond our natural understanding that we just have to let the Holy Spirit travail through us. It's very important to remember that in the kingdom of God there is no birth without travail, just as in the natural order.

SPIRIT-LED PRAYER AND FASTING

Lord, enable and fill me with your compassion for the needs of other believers, for those you have called to your kingdom, for leaders in the secular world, and for the servants of the church. Enable me to pray in the Spirit and with my understanding of all things that are of the highest concern to you.

Pray for God's perfect will to be done in our lives and in the lives of our family and friends.

Father, I ask that your Holy Spirit would show me how to pray in accordance with your perfect will for <insert friend or family member's name>. Empower me to pray in the Spirit and give me your assurance that you will answer our prayers according to your will. I ask for your sovereign grace to soften our hearts to surrender unconditionally to your plan. In time open our eyes to see, understand, and accept your will.

Pray for those who have been sent out for the sake of the Name.

God, I do not know how to pray as I should; but you know every aspect of all things that concern us. Speak to my spirit, impress upon my mind what you want me to intercede for. I hold up <insert friend or family member's name> with my prayers, even as Aaron and Hur held up the arms of Moses until Israel prevailed (Exodus 17:12).

Pray for God's kingdom to come and his will to be done on earth as it is in heaven.

Lord, I will pray in the Spirit and with my understanding that the thing I do not even know to ask might be accomplished in your perfect time and place.

Allow a genuine burden of the Holy Spirit to lead you to intercede.

Lord, enable and fill me with your compassion for the needs of other believers, for those you have called to your kingdom, for leaders in the secular world, and for the servants of the church. Enable me to pray in the Spirit and with my understanding of all things that are of the highest concern to you.

CHAPTER NINE

STANDING IN THE GAP

"I searched for a man among them who would build up a wall and stand in the gap before Me for the land, so that I would not destroy it; but I found no one."

—EZEKIEL 22:30 (NASB)

Intercession is the act of intervening between two or more parties in an attempt to bring reconciliation. God "through Christ reconciled us to himself and gave us the ministry of reconciliation" (2 Corinthians 5:18). Whether you are praying, preaching the gospel, showing mercy, or simply demonstrating God's love through random and sometimes extraordinary acts of kindness, it's all a part of that chief calling—the ministry of reconciliation. There are all kinds of things we can pray for or against—for nations, for the spread of the gospel, for spiritual power and perseverance—but almost always, it comes down to intercession for people.

Praying for Muslims

In 2014, we started praying for opportunities to reach the largest Muslim community of a major city in Southeast Asia. For security reasons, names of those involved and details about the city will not be disclosed. Jonathan led an outreach team of ten to this community, including five Muslim students who are disciples (in Arabic, *hawariyyun*) of Jesus Christ (*Isa al-Masih*). For many years, churches and other Christian organizations had prayed for open doors to this community, where preaching the gospel had always been a challenge.

The door that opened for the team was a direct result of intense fasting and intercession. A year before this, a group of rebel fighters associated with a radical group claiming to be Muslim launched an attack and took over this major city. Many of the local citizens who did not support them were killed or executed. Government forces finally regained control after several months of fighting, and the militants (including many members of their extended family) were detained in a maximum-security prison. All of the militants were awaiting their trials.

A high official of the jail facility was a believer who had been petitioning God and talking to Christian organizations for workers who could help engage and minister to these families. He believed that only through the love of Jesus Christ could these families' lives be truly transformed. Not reaching out to them could also lead to greater extremist influence inside the correctional facility.

Jonathan and his team had been working with an association which gathered different churches and missionary agencies in continually praying for Muslims. In one of their collaboration meetings with leaders of different agencies, they were introduced to this jail official, who initially gave them access to the militant group and families in prison.

First, the team was given the chance to conduct the sessions with twenty prison guards to acquaint them with what would be taught. After two sessions with the guards, the team began meeting with four inmates who were combatants from different militant groups in the country and were willing to listen to our team. But those meetings ended suddenly when the assistant warden, who was a devout Muslim, convinced the warden to require more official paperwork from us.

When this door closed, another one opened to serve the women's prison. These women were part of a large extended family of the militant group, most of whom were awaiting trial for their roles in the violent take-over of the city. The female warden was also hesitant at first. However, when the high jail official witnessed a conversation between Jonathan and the matriarch of the fighters' family, he decided to give our team an opportunity to serve the women. When the matriarch asked Jonathan who we were, he quoted a passage from the Qur'an, Surah 3:52—a verse that identified them as disciples of Jesus Christ.

This simple introduction with reference to the Qur'an made an impact on her, and she said that she was looking forward to the team's visit. The female warden also told us that this large family was the only Muslim group in her assigned prison who did not receive any help from the outside and that these women needed groceries and hygiene kits. Over the next four months, the team provided for their needs and led discussions that incorporated gospel-centered leadership principles. This became the opportunity for them to demonstrate the love of Jesus to the families.

The women were well-versed in Arabic, Sharia Law, and the Qur'an. Ministering to them each week for four months was not easy. At first, the women were adamant that Jesus was just a prophet and that it was blasphemy for them to pray in his name. The team members felt the tension whenever discussing verses from the Bible (*Kitab* or literally "the book"), since these women questioned its authenticity.

Jonathan and the team continued to trust in the Lord as they prayed, fasted, and ministered together. Many other intercessors prayed and fasted with them every week for the entire four months. In the course of time, they saw the power of the Holy Spirit opening the hearts of the women prisoners. They were amazed at how frequently the Holy Spirit gave them supernatural wisdom to answer questions and pray for women much older than they were.

Since Muslim men are allowed to have multiple wives and families, the scope and relationships among the extended family groups are complicated and difficult for those outside their culture to comprehend. In particular, the family matriarch (the first wife of the patriarch) was a tremendous help for the team. She would often stand up in the midst of a heated discussion and tell all the women in the family to calm down. She said that if they are to be a bridge, they needed to also read the Bible, since, like the Qur'an to them, this is what the disciples of Jesus based their lives upon. One woman, a suspect in a high-profile criminal trial, was an influential government official, a granddaughter of a sultan, and a passionate Muslim. She said she approved of the discussions since it was part of Allah's plan. What a drastic change for these women—from heated discussions to accepting the reading of the Bible!

The women slowly began to see that Jonathan's team had come to serve, not convert them. They eventually loosened up in the group discussions when the team said they were helping because Matthew 5:44 said to love your enemy, which baffled them. Their fellow Muslims cursed them and wanted them dead, but Jonathan's team prayed for them and declared blessings over them. Serving these women delivered the message of unconditional love taught by Jesus in the Scriptures.

The young women in the group kept asking questions about life and faith. One of them, Iman, prayed in one of the small groups. Muslims typically pray memorized Arabic prayers, but this time, Iman was able to utter her own personal prayer. They all eventually became comfortable in praying in the name of Jesus Christ.

At one of the discussions, the team showed from the Scriptures that God's name was Yahweh, not Allah, and he became flesh in *Isa al-Masih*. The matriarch's younger sister asked, "So are you saying that Allah and *Isa al-Masih* are the same?"

For a Muslim to even ask such a question is already a breakthrough, and it was followed up with another that was equally amazing:

"If they are indeed the same, why did he allow bad people to kill him?"

There was a pause in the discussion that seemed to last for minutes as the questions hung in the air of the prison meeting room. The team was praying silently and asking the Holy Spirit to intervene. The family matriarch finally stood up.

"He was not killed," she said. "He gave his life."

All the women remained silent, and the team members were astounded. They hadn't taught them that. The Holy Spirit was indeed speaking to the hearts of these women. When the team prayed, the matriarch exclaimed, "Praise *Isa al-Masih*."

As they closed their time together, the team declared salvation to those who believed and received Jesus in their hearts. There was rejoicing in the air. The matriarchs from three different tribes hugged one another and laughed together—a very uncommon sight! They even hugged each of our team members before they left. Because of the impact of this experience, the team was allowed to visit once a month for the next year. The matriarchs of two other family groups told the team that when they were released, they would gather their people so they too could hear about the gospel.

. . .

There is a long tradition of intercession in both the Old and New Testaments. Moses was one of the most prolific intercessors in the Old Testament. His first intercessory effort on behalf of the children of Israel was in the aftermath of the forging of the golden calf. The beginning of the story is recorded in Exodus 32:8–14:

> *"They have turned aside quickly out of the way that I commanded them. They have made for themselves a golden calf and have worshiped it and sacrificed to it and said, 'These are your gods, O Israel, who brought you up out of the land of Egypt!'" And the LORD said to Moses, "I have seen this people, and behold, it is a stiff-necked people. **Now therefore let me alone, that my wrath may burn hot against them and I may consume them, in order that I may make a great nation of you.**"*
>
> *But Moses implored the LORD his God and said, "O LORD, why does your wrath burn hot against your people, whom you have brought out of the land of Egypt with great power and with a mighty hand? Why should the Egyptians say, 'With evil intent did he bring them out, to kill them in the mountains and to consume them from the face of the earth'?*
>
> *"**Turn from your burning anger and relent from this disaster against your people.** Remember Abraham, Isaac, and Israel, your servants, to whom you swore by your own self, and said to them, 'I will multiply your offspring as the stars of heaven, and all*

this land that I have promised I will give to your offspring, and they shall inherit it forever.'"

And the LORD relented *from the disaster that he had spoken of bringing on his people.*

There are several important things to note about the mercy of God and the effectiveness of intercession. On this occasion and several others, Moses resisted the temptation to seek his own benefit but stood in the gap between a very angry God and a very obstinate, rebellious people. One of the often overlooked aspects of the divine character is what seems to be an overwhelming persuasiveness that sincere intercession has upon God. It's strange and awkward speaking of God being overwhelmed by anything. However, God's mercy in response to selfless intercession seems to be (or at least is portrayed in this passage as) almost irresistible to God, whose love and mercy are described as being "as high as the heavens are above the earth" (Psalm 103:11). God says to Moses, ". . . let me alone, that my wrath may burn hot against them and I may consume them . . ." In other words, he was saying, "Don't intercede for them; don't plead for me to have mercy on them; don't remind me of my promise; don't ask me to change my mind." But Moses did intercede, and God did relent. The NASB (1995) says, ". . . the LORD changed His mind . . ." Actually, I believe God's intention all along was to show his great mercy. However, it was required that someone stand in the gap between God and those in such desperate need of mercy, grace, and forgiveness.

That need or requirement for intercessors to stand in the gap and the consequences of their absence is stated again in this passage:

"The people of the land have practiced extortion and committed robbery, and they have oppressed the poor and needy, and have oppressed the stranger without justice. **I searched for a man among them who would build up a wall and stand in the gap before Me for the land, so that I would not destroy it;**

but I found no one. So I have poured out My indignation on them; I have consumed them with the fire of My wrath; I have brought their way upon their heads," declares the Lord GOD.
—EZEKIEL 22:29–31 (NASB)

The responsibility of intercessors who have embraced the ministry of reconciliation is expressed through the prophet Isaiah: "The LORD saw it, and it displeased him that there was no justice. He saw that **there was no man**, and **wondered that there was no one to intercede**" (Isaiah 59:15–16). Perhaps, God is still wondering.

This mediatorial work on behalf of God's people is again stated unequivocally by the prophet Samuel: "For the LORD will not forsake his people, for his great name's sake, because it has pleased the LORD to make you a people for himself. Moreover, as for me, far be it from me that I should **sin against the LORD** by ceasing to pray for you . . ." (1 Samuel 12:22–24).

There are other examples of effective intercession in the Scriptures. On two occasions, Moses was compelled to stand in the gap between God's anger and the children of Israel (Numbers 14, 21). In Genesis 18, Abram bargained with God on behalf of Lot and the cities of Sodom and Gomorrah. In 1 Samuel 25:17–19, Abigail intercedes on behalf of her stupid husband, Nabal, who had so greatly offended King David. Ezra, Daniel, and Nehemiah all interceded for God's covenant people by first identifying (assuming or taking on) the guilt of the nation as their own (Ezra 9:6–15; Nehemiah 1:3–11; Daniel 9:4–19).

The greatest demonstration of intercession for sinners is in Isaiah 53, the prophecy of the coming Messiah who would stand in the gap, bearing the sin of many and reconciling us to God.

*Out of the anguish of his soul he shall see and be satisfied; by his knowledge shall the righteous one, my servant, make many to be **accounted righteous**, and he shall **bear their iniquities**. Therefore I will divide him a portion with the many, and he shall*

*divide the spoil with the strong, because he poured out his soul to death and was numbered with the transgressors; yet **he bore the sin of many, and makes intercession for the transgressors.***
—ISAIAH 53:11–12

This passage reveals that Jesus Christ is the ultimate intercessor, the one who stood in the gap between the righteous, holy God and sinful, rebellious man to bring reconciliation through his sacrificial death and resurrection. Even more amazing, our Lord Jesus Christ continues this intercessory ministry in heaven to this very day as our great High Priest. As Hebrews 7:25 says, "Consequently, he is able to save to the uttermost those who draw near to God through him, since he always lives to make intercession for them."

What then is the purpose of prayer and intercession in light of this truth? Dutch Sheets, in his seminal book *Intercessory Prayer*, asserts that our prayers and intercession are primarily an extension of this mediatorial work of Christ.[1] Our prayers are fueled by the knowledge that God has invited us to partner with him in this vital ministry, as Jesus taught us in the Lord's prayer. The apostle Paul reminds us that we are ambassadors for Christ, who longs to reconcile the world to himself (2 Corinthians 5:20). Christ's great longing is expressed through our fervent prayers and bold gospel proclamation, bringing forth salvation and the restoration of our relationship with him.

· · ·

"Jesus came into Galilee, proclaiming the gospel of God, and saying, 'The time is fulfilled, and the kingdom of God is at hand; repent and believe in the gospel'" (Mark 1:14–16). Becoming a part of the kingdom of God requires responding to the gospel. The initial challenges are two-fold: repenting of our enmity toward God and turning to faith in him. I know this is basic to our understanding of the gospel, but it's an essential part of intercession.

First of all, each time one intercedes for an unbeliever, it is as if he or she is standing in the gap of a broken relationship or between warring parties who are at enmity with one another. Most unbelievers would not admit they are enemies and may not even be aware of it. However, many who feel neither love nor hatred toward God are indifferent to him because they don't know who he is or what he is like. They neither understand his love and judgment nor the depth of their sin and his sacrifice for our redemption. If they were to become aware of his demand for absolute surrender to his Lordship in all things, and if they were to sense the price they would pay for rejecting him as their King, they would more likely vent their rage and anger in the vilest ways, becoming (in the words of Jonathan Edwards) "like vipers, hissing and spitting poison at God."[2]

Mankind's enmity against God and his demand for repentance is expressed throughout the Scriptures, one particular passage being Psalm 2:

> *Why do the nations rage*
> * and the peoples plot in vain?*
> *The kings of the earth set themselves,*
> * and the rulers take counsel together,*
> * against the LORD and against his Anointed, saying,*
> *"Let us burst their bonds apart*
> * and cast away their cords from us."*
>
> *He who sits in the heavens laughs;*
> * the Lord holds them in derision.*
> *Then he will speak to them in his wrath,*
> * and terrify them in his fury, saying,*
> *"As for me, I have set my King*
> * on Zion, my holy hill."*
> *I will tell of the decree:*
> * The LORD said to me, "You are my Son;*
> * today I have begotten you.*

Ask of me, and I will make the nations your heritage,
 and the ends of the earth your possession.
You shall break them with a rod of iron
 and dash them in pieces like a potter's vessel."
Now therefore, O kings, be wise;
 be warned, O rulers of the earth.
Serve the LORD with fear,
 and rejoice with trembling.
Kiss the Son,
 lest he be angry, and you perish in the way,
 for his wrath is quickly kindled.
Blessed are all who take refuge in him.

Secondly, there is the matter of faith. Many high-minded intellectuals often vent their rage against injustice and use their argument as a reason for either their unbelief or their enmity. "If there is a God and that God is good," they argue, "then why is there so much injustice in the world? Either God is a cruel dictator, and I hate him, or there is no God to believe in." If however, one "chooses" unbelief, then there is no such thing as justice or injustice, good or evil—only the survival of the fittest.

The idea of God and the gospel puts all of mankind in an inescapable dilemma. Think about it for a moment—how can people be convinced that the man Jesus of Nazareth is the incarnation of God, has risen from the dead, and desires to fill us with his Spirit; that his presence and power are a reality in this world almost 2,000 years after he was born in the little town of Bethlehem; and that we can actually have a living relationship with the God of the universe?

To believe in God is no greater leap of faith than to believe there is no God. To a large extent, it depends on which way one chooses to leap. But what would cause a person to leap toward God, to be transformed from a doubter and an enemy to a worshiper and a believer? It would take a miracle.

• • •

Jesus told his future apostolic evangelists about how that miracle would happen over and over, many millions of times. "I will ask the Father, and he will give you another Helper, to be with you forever, even the Spirit of truth, whom the world cannot receive, **because it neither sees him nor knows him**. You know him, for he dwells with you and will be in you" (John 14:16–17).

Unbelievers do not believe because they do not see him and do not know him. In other words, they do not believe because they are blinded to the reality of his presence, and for that reason, the Holy Spirit was given to us as our Helper. Even Jesus himself, preaching and performing miracles, did not cause men and women to believe unless they had been given the grace to do so.

> *Though he had done so many signs before them, **they still did not believe** in him, so that the word spoken by the prophet Isaiah might be fulfilled: "Lord, who has believed what he heard from us, and to whom has the arm of the Lord been revealed?" Therefore **they could not believe**. For again Isaiah said, "**He has blinded their eyes and hardened their heart**, lest they see with their eyes, and understand with their heart, and turn, and I would heal them."*
> —JOHN 12:37–40

> *And even if our gospel is veiled, it is veiled to those who are perishing. In their case the god of this world has **blinded the minds of the unbelievers**, to keep them from seeing the light of the gospel of the glory of Christ, who is the image of God.*
> —2 CORINTHIANS 4:3–4

Even those who are convinced of the existence of God and the resurrection of Jesus are only born again because their eyes have been opened.

They have been given a gift of faith to believe and the grace to repent. This reality is affirmed throughout the New Testament.

> *They said, "Is not this Jesus, the son of Joseph, whose father and mother we know? How does he now say, 'I have come down from heaven'?" Jesus answered them, "Do not grumble among yourselves. **No one can come to me unless the Father who sent me draws him.** And I will raise him up on the last day."*
>
> —JOHN 6:42–44

> *He said to them, "But who do you say that I am?" Simon Peter replied, "You are the Christ, the Son of the living God." And Jesus answered him, "Blessed are you, Simon Bar-Jonah! **For flesh and blood has not revealed this to you, but my Father who is in heaven.**"*
>
> —MATTHEW 16:15–17

Jesus described how the Holy Spirit helps in bringing unbelievers to faith and repentance:

> *"Nevertheless, I tell you the truth: it is to your advantage that I go away, for if I do not go away, the Helper will not come to you. But if I go, I will send him to you. And when he comes, **he will convict the world concerning sin and righteousness and judgment**: concerning sin, because they do not believe in me; concerning righteousness, because I go to the Father, and **you will see me no longer**; concerning judgment, because the ruler of this world is judged."*
>
> —JOHN 16:7–11

None of that happens without the Holy Spirit revealing his presence and power, and more often than we realize, it is because someone has been interceding for them. That was the case with me and the prayers of my mother.

Fasting and Praying for Unbelievers

Pray that God would grant unbelievers the grace to repent.

The supernatural empowering of the Holy Spirit is what enables a person to overcome the powers of sin and Satan that have firmly established the self on the throne. No one truly surrenders to the Lordship of Christ without the grace to do so. The addiction to serving self is too powerful to escape. Apart from that grace, a person will eventually return to their old way of life.

> **PRAYER FOR UNBELIEVERS**
>
> *I pray for <insert friend or family member's names>, that the Holy Spirit would convict them of sin, righteousness, and judgment to come (John 16:8). Reveal your love to them. Draw them to yourself and grant them the grace to repent and follow you as disciples.*

Pray that the Holy Spirit would take the blinders off the eyes of the unbelieving.

Jun Escosar and Ferdie Cabiling are two of my dear friends in ministry. They are both evangelists and share how they pray before preaching a sermon, taking someone through *One2One*, leading a small group, or simply preaching the gospel. They both said without hesitation: "I pray that the Holy Spirit will open their eyes." They know from countless experiences that no one comes to saving faith in Jesus Christ by intellectual assent. It only happens when the Holy Spirit awakens them to the reality of God's love and mercy.

> **PRAYER FOR UNBELIEVERS**
>
> *I pray that you open the eyes of <insert friend or family member's names> and give them an acute awareness of the truth of your existence, of the nearness of your presence, of the sin that separates them from you. Give them the grace to believe and receive the gift of righteousness by faith.*

Pray for wisdom and timely words.

Jesus told his disciples, "When they bring you before the synagogues and the rulers and the authorities, do not be anxious about how you should defend yourself or what you should say, for the Holy Spirit will teach you in that very hour what you ought to say" (Luke 12:11–12). Sometimes the wisdom of what you ought to say comes to mind so clearly that it is as astounding to you as it is to unbelievers. That was the case with the team that preached the gospel to a group of radical fighters in the women's prison.

Other times, we have no sense of any divine inspiration and are left speechless. On many of those occasions, instead of remaining silent, we should simply step out in faith, believing that God's word "shall not return to me empty, but it shall accomplish that which I purpose, and shall succeed in the thing for which I sent it" (Isaiah 55:11).

> **PRAYER FOR UNBELIEVERS**
>
> *I pray that your Holy Spirit will give me wisdom and the perfect words to speak whenever I engage unbelievers in conversations about Jesus. Enable me to walk in wisdom toward outsiders, making the best use of the time (Ephesians 5:16). Let my speech always be gracious, seasoned with salt, so that I may know how I ought to answer each person (Colossians 4:5–6).*

Pray that God would grant unbelievers the grace to repent.

I pray for <insert friend or family member's names>, that the Holy Spirit would convict them of sin, righteousness, and judgment to come (John 16:8). Reveal your love to them. Draw them to yourself and grant them the grace to repent and follow you as disciples.

Pray that the Holy Spirit would take the blinders off the eyes of the unbelieving.

I pray that you open the eyes of <insert friend or family member's names> and give them an acute awareness of the truth of your existence, of the nearness of your presence, of the sin that separates them from you. Give them the grace to believe and receive the gift of righteousness by faith.

Pray for wisdom and timely words.

I pray that your Holy Spirit will give me wisdom and the perfect words to speak whenever I engage unbelievers in conversations about Jesus. Enable me to walk in wisdom toward outsiders, making the best use of the time (Ephesians 5:16). Let my speech always be gracious, seasoned with salt, so that I may know how I ought to answer each person (Colossians 4:5–6).

CHAPTER TEN

INTENTIONAL APPROACH TO INTERCESSION

First of all, then, I urge that supplications, prayers, intercessions, and thanksgivings be made for all people, for kings and all who are in high positions . . .

—1 TIMOTHY 2:1–2

In 1996, twelve years after the initial launch of Victory, small group leaders met every month for Vision, Instruction, and Prayer. This VIP meeting emphasized praying for and reaching out to unsaved relatives and friends. Each leader was encouraged to write these names down on a VIP list—very important persons—and pray for salvation, healing, provision, and guidance for them every day. Decades later, we're still making lists and interceding for people in need.

Jun Escosar and his wife, Gigi, were making their VIP list in preparation for a Victory group they were going to lead—the names of the Victory members on one side of a bookmark and the names of ten unsaved friends or relatives on the other side.

"I only wrote down two unsaved friends," Jun commented. "I'd become so far removed from my old friends. Struggling to come up with names of ten unsaved people for my VIP list, I became very convicted about those I had left behind without a witness to the gospel. But the names of unsaved relatives easily came to mind. Between the two of us at that time, we had a lot of unsaved relatives."

Gigi's uncle, Tony Salva, was a prominent lawyer in Manila and head of the legal department for the Buddhist Association of the Philippines. He acknowledged years later that he had been proud, rich, and a self-proclaimed skeptic about anything having to do with Christianity. If there was any person farther away from God or a more impossible case, this might have been it.

"I debated with myself about adding him to our VIP list," Jun said. "I would say to myself, *It's a leap of faith that is too far.* Then I would remember, *All things are possible with God.* Finally, I said to Gigi, 'Let's not just include people who are easy to pray for; let's believe for the impossible. No one is beyond the reach of the power of God.' So, we started praying."

In Jun's mental debate, faith in God's mercy and the power of prayer won out over his fear of disappointment.

Several weeks after Jun and Gigi began praying for Mr. Salva, he visited the US and was hosted by relatives who were Christians. In deference to their hospitality, Mr. Salva felt he had no choice but to accept their invitation to attend church on Sunday morning. He reluctantly agreed to go and sat through the service, counting minutes until he could escape. He hated the church because he felt the institution was a racket, extorting money from people with the promise that God would reward the faithful followers with eternal life.

The family went to a nice restaurant after service, but when Mr. Salva realized the conversation was going to be more talk about God and the church, he excused himself and walked out. With time to kill, he began browsing through books for sale at a kiosk in the mall. He eventually picked up a book by a Jewish Ph.D. that attacked the claims of Jesus, charging that he had deliberately set out to fulfill the messianic prophecies. That argument didn't get any traction with Mr. Salva's mental cross-examination because, though Jesus may have had motive, he did not possess the means to fulfill the claims—that is, prophetic fulfillments that were beyond his control. What did astound him was the realization that Jesus of Nazareth was not at all a mythical figure but an actual historical person. He went back immediately to the lunch and asked his wife, "Don't we have a nephew who's a pastor? I want to meet him the moment we get back to Manila."

Jun continues, "I hadn't spoken to Gigi's uncle in seven years and only met him once or twice. But about a month after Gigi and I began praying, he called and wanted to talk with me about leading a Bible study with his family and him. Gigi and I were dumbfounded—but what should I have expected? I went to see Auntie Pilar and Uncle Tony the following week and preached the gospel with their whole family gathered around the dining room table."

Mr. Salva asked, "Why have I been deprived of this story all my life?"

As a result, everyone in the Salva family made a decision to trust Christ as their Savior, all their children got connected in Victory groups, and they have become some of Victory's most generous givers. No one is beyond the reach of the power of God.

• • •

Even though some of our leaders have now been in ministry for several decades, the early desperation of those college students is still there. Many of us can still remember offering bags that jingled because they contained only a few coins, praying that celebrities on billboards would one day get saved and discipled in our church, or sacrificially giving meager savings for the purchase of our church's first property.

Victory planting churches sometimes makes me think of how Jollibee puts up fast-food restaurants across the nation. The Philippines is, after all, one of the few nations where a local chain like Jollibee has hundreds of stores and goes neck and neck with McDonald's.

Over the years, Victory has grown so much that it also sometimes feels like we're the crew of a 300,000-ton oil tanker. In an emergency, that tanker would require headway of more than a mile to make a 180-degree turn and ten miles to stop. Thinking that far ahead to anticipate problems, needs, and pitfalls tends to keep us on our knees. More than anything else, what motivates us to undergird everything with prayer is knowing that as a leadership team we're in way over our heads. With a lot of prayer and fasting, we have at times wrestled some monumental problems to the ground. We've also had the painful experience of needing to course correct: focusing on addressing leadership gaps rather than prioritizing church attendance, which Pastor Steve and William Murrell wrote about in *The Multiplication Challenge.*[1]

I don't know if we are more or less desperate than any other church. I do feel that our commitment to prayer and dependence upon God is a direct result of our profound sense of need. Each congregation that attempts to go into all the world to make disciples for Christ—regardless of the size, location, or stage of development—has plenty of reasons to be desperate for the empowering presence of the Holy Spirit. Like Moses said to God, "If your presence will not go with me, do not bring us up from here" (Exodus 33:15).

Methodical Approach to Prayer and Fasting

Ingrained into the ethos of our movement is our ongoing commitment to prayer, evangelism, and discipleship—generally in that order. Prayer is the first order of business in any and every Victory initiative. Intercession prepares the soil, the word of God is the seed we plant, and mature disciples are the fruit. We also learned early on that prayer, coupled with fasting, had the power to loose people from the bonds of demonic power and spiritual strongholds, thus opening their minds and hearts to the gospel (Isaiah 58:6; Mark 9:29). Consequently, it has become an essential first step in our church growth through small-group evangelism.

As I said in chapter 6, our discipleship journey has been constantly tweaked, evaluated, and finely tuned over the years. We make disciples by engaging culture and community, establishing biblical foundations, equipping believers to minister, and empowering disciples to make disciples. Our objective is to proceed to empowering as soon as possible in order for each new believer to reach their unsaved family and friends. The following is explained in our *Making Disciples* classes:

1. Identify two or three believers who desire to make disciples by reaching the lost. Together, make a list of people you can invite to a Victory group. Meet once a week for one month with these believers to prepare for the Victory group you want to start. On the days you will meet, it would be good to fast, share the vision of making disciples together, and pray for those you want to invite to the Victory group. **Pray for those on your VIP List.** If you are the only believer you know of in your family, campus, or workplace, start by doing *One2One* with a friend or family member. Once you have done *One2One* with two or three already, you may start a Victory group by bringing these believers together. You can jump-start a group once you have four members, and the Victory group will grow as the four of you pray for and reach out to lost family members, friends, and acquaintances.

2. Include your lost family members, friends, and acquaintances in your circle to lead them to God. Intentionally build relationships with people and get to know them. Believe God for opportunities to invite your family members and friends to your Victory group.

3. Intercede for them. **Pray for the lost**, and even those who are not actively involved in church yet. **Pray regularly** for their salvation, and for opportunities to share your two-minute miracle, and preach the gospel. **Pray specifically** for God to meet their needs and draw them closer to him.

4. Invite them to your Victory group. Engage the people you are praying for. Apply the SALT principle: Start a conversation, Ask questions, Listen, and Tell the story. Get to know them and build relationships with them. As the opportunities arise, share your two-minute miracle and preach the gospel. Be in faith as you invite them to the Victory group. Remember to be clear and specific about the time, date, and place of your Victory group, and remind them to come beforehand. Believe that God will cause your Victory group to grow, and together you will honor him and make disciples.

That's what we teach in the *Making Disciples* class. What usually happens is a bit more intense. Why the difference? If we began mandating aspects of spiritual disciplines like prayer and fasting, we would be starting down a path toward a form of legalism we have tried to avoid. Our objective is to see church members inspired and empowered by the Holy Spirit to intercede for those they are inviting to the Victory group. These evangelistic Bible studies usually begin with a leader and two or three new believers who are a few steps ahead in their discipleship journey. Once a week, they fast and meet to agree in prayer for those on their list. They do this for four weeks, and by the third week, they each begin inviting people on their VIP lists to be part of the Victory group. Throughout the years, we have launched discipleship campaigns that have resulted in new Victory groups, new Victory group leaders being empowered by the Holy Spirit, and new believers being established in the faith.

What works for us in the Philippines may not work as well in another cultural context. However, the undeniable and inescapable reality is that **nothing works in any cultural setting** without a commitment to intercession, prayer, and fasting for unbelievers to be birthed into the kingdom of God.

· · ·

Prayer is not simply a means to engage the help of the Holy Spirit to get people to come to a Bible study or even to convict them of their need to be born again. We know of many occasions in which the prayer request of an invitee has left unbelievers and new believers astounded at the demonstration of God's power and grace.

Princess Punzalan is a famous Filipino actress and the sister of Paolo Punzalan, our Victory Fort senior pastor. She has starred in over a dozen movies and many television shows. She won Best New TV Personality in 1987 and Best Actress for her roles in *From the Heart* (1998) and *At the End of Eternity* (1990). In the early years of Victory, when we transitioned to small groups, Princess joined a small group Bible study with some friends. Most of the people in the group were not yet (but soon to be) believers. These meetings always ended with a time of prayer. Princess explains what happened in one meeting.

> One Wednesday night, there was this girl who was seated next to me, who was also a new believer. I asked her if she had any prayer requests. She said, "Nothing really, but if my father is still alive, it would be great if he would get in touch with us." Her father had gone missing or had simply walked out on his wife and children. No one had seen or heard from him in sixteen years. We all prayed for her father to get in touch with them. Nothing loud or dramatic, just conversational prayer. We just prayed in faith for the seemingly impossible request and believed that God heard us. If her father was still alive, God would bring him home.

There were half a dozen reasons the father's return might not be a good idea. In fact, it could have been a disastrous encounter for them all. But that was in God's hands. The group was just responding to a new believer's great sense of loss and disappointment with a prayer of faith. Princess continues:

> Amazingly, three days had not gone by before her father suddenly showed up in their home. He was compelled by the Holy Spirit to return, and with the help of the girl's uncle had returned to their city, stood at the door, and reluctantly knocked. The uncle, who

lived in the same city, had known his brother's whereabouts for all those years.

It took some time, but they experienced reconciliation in their family. Her father may not have gone back to live with them again, but they learned to accept her father's new family. She was able to forgive. Before he passed away, she visited her father with his other children.

Princess recalls:

This story encouraged me so much! The Lord hears our prayers and answers them. He is so present in the lives of his children. This girl is still walking with God and has been reaching out to preach the gospel to her newly found siblings.

Obviously, this is not something you can schedule into your small group Bible study—as if we were to write into the manual, "On the third Wednesday, conclude the meeting with a miracle." The more important takeaway is that those small group leaders were predisposed to pray and believe. In other words, when challenges to faith and prayer emerged, they were more likely to lean into the challenge than run from it. And what if God chose not to answer that prayer; if the father never reappeared; if he had been dead for over a decade? The power, purposes, and prerogative, as well as the timing of God's response, rest with him, not with us. It is simply our responsibility to pray and believe all things are possible. We've tried to encourage our people, particularly our small group leaders, to welcome the opportunity to pray and fast for the seemingly impossible, because it only takes faith the size of a mustard seed.

Intercession for Ongoing Discipleship

It is presumptuous to believe that God will automatically recover those who are lost, make disciples of the nations, and raise up leaders apart from our intercessory prayers. Consequently, prayer is our first order of business. That was probably the most important lesson I learned from the church-planting initiative in Quezon City. We did almost nothing but pray and fast for the campus community for the first six months.

We assume that all the 4Es of our discipleship strategy need to be undergirded with prayer and fasting. We pray for people to be engaged by the gospel and receive Jesus as their Lord, to be established in the faith to stand firm against the temptations of the enemy, to be equipped to win others to Christ, and to be empowered for leadership. It takes more than well-designed discipleship programs. New disciples progress as other believers support them in prayer. Jesus said to Peter on the eve of his denial:

> *"Simon, Simon, behold, Satan demanded **to have you**, that he might **sift you** like wheat, but I have prayed for you that your faith may not fail. And when you have turned again, strengthen your brothers." Peter said to him, "Lord, I am ready to go with you both to prison and to death." Jesus said, "I tell you, Peter, the rooster will not crow this day, until you deny three times that you know me."*
> **— LUKE 22:31–34**

This is remarkably similar to Satan's demand to put Job to the test (Job 1:6–12). There are at least two overarching truths in these verses: Satan's opposition to discipleship doesn't end when an individual decides to follow Jesus. And, if Jesus felt compelled to intercede for Peter's continued spiritual growth, how much more should we continue to pray for new believers? Some might say that Peter and his fellow apostles were special people in unusual circumstances. But would you consider the women imprisoned along with their husbands mentioned in the previous chapter to be in an easier circumstance? Or is their continued growth in the faith less dependent on God's grace and our intercession? And who can know which of those new believers will turn out to be a great evangelist, pastor, or apologist?

The prophets wrote, "I searched for a man among them who would build up a wall and stand in the gap before Me for the land, so that I would not destroy it; but I found no one" (Ezekiel 22:30, NASB); "He saw that there was no man, and wondered that there was no one to intercede" (Isaiah 59:16).

Programmed Intercession

Pray and fast for the nations and the lost. Pray that spiritual growth will not be an annual event, but a lifestyle.

That was made abundantly clear by Jesus in the parable of the sower. The word of God (the seed) fell on different soil conditions. The fertility of the soil never seemed to matter, only if it had been unprepared or untended. The parable of the sower is a prescription for ongoing intercession, that the word of God would bear fruit a hundredfold in the lives of new believers.

> **PRAYER FOR NEW BELIEVERS**
> *I pray for all those who are new in the faith: that you strengthen their resolve to follow you with consecrated hearts, that you protect them from the attacks and temptations of the evil one, that you give them a hunger for your word, and that you fill and empower them with your Holy Spirit.*

Pray for unbelievers and expect God to answer as a sign of his presence and power.

One of the easiest ways to engage unbelievers is to simply ask, "Do you pray?" You're sure to get some awkward answers, especially with the follow-up question, "Can I pray for you about something that is of great concern to you?" If they are unbelievers, nominal, or even radical followers of another religion, God wants to reveal himself to them. Sometimes I think that the farther away people are from God, the more likely he is to demonstrate his power in astounding ways—as was the case with the girl in Princess's story. It is not uncommon for Muslims to become followers of Jesus as a result of praying for God to reveal himself to them. Prayer is not only part of the preparation for evangelism but also a way to witness to others.

> **PRAYER FOR UNBELIEVERS AND NEW BELIEVERS**
> *Lord, look upon their threats and grant your servants to continue to speak your word with all boldness, while you stretch out your hand to heal, and signs and wonders are performed through the name of your holy servant Jesus (Acts 4:29–30). I pray that you, the God of all grace, would call them to your eternal glory in Christ, and perfect, confirm, strengthen, and establish them (1 Peter 5:10).*

Pray for the conversions that seem impossible, not just the ones that are probable.

Jesus made statements about faith that were both encouraging and perplexing:

> *The apostles said to the Lord, "Increase our faith!" And the Lord said, "If you had faith like a grain of mustard seed, you could say to this mulberry tree, 'Be uprooted and planted in the sea,' and it would obey you."*
>
> —LUKE 17:5-6

Jesus defined mountain-moving faith as being so easy that even a child could do it—that it was not the size of faith but the willingness to ask. Children don't hesitate to ask because they're not sophisticated enough to calculate the difficulty of the answered prayer. In other words, they have not learned how to doubt. You rarely know how long or how intensely the Holy Spirit has been dealing with a person. Don't just intercede for those who are "not far from the kingdom of God" (Mark 12:34), but pray with expectation for those who do not even seem close.

PRAYER FOR UNBELIEVERS

I pray for <insert friend or family member's names> who seem to be so far from your kingdom, so indifferent to their need for grace and forgiveness, so reliant on their own righteousness, and yet so entangled in their sinful nature. Lord, I intercede on their behalf. Relying on the sacrifice of your Son, I ask that you extend your mercy, snatch them from the power of Satan, and redeem them according to your purpose.

Pray and fast for the nations and the lost. Pray that spiritual growth will not be an annual event, but a lifestyle.

I pray for all those who are new in the faith: that you strengthen their resolve to follow you with consecrated hearts, that you protect them from the attacks and temptations of the evil one, that you give them a hunger for your word, and that you fill and empower them with your Holy Spirit.

Pray for unbelievers and expect God to answer as a sign of his presence and power.

Lord, look upon their threats and grant your servants to continue to speak your word with all boldness, while you stretch out your hand to heal, and signs and wonders are performed through the name of your holy servant Jesus (Acts 4:29–30). I pray that you, the God of all grace, would call them to your eternal glory in Christ, and perfect, confirm, strengthen, and establish them (1 Peter 5:10).

Pray for the conversions that seem impossible, not just the ones that are probable.

I pray for <insert friend or family member's names> who seem to be so far from your kingdom, so indifferent to their need for grace and forgiveness, so reliant on their own righteousness, and yet so entangled in their sinful nature. Lord, I intercede on their behalf. Relying on the sacrifice of your Son, I ask that you extend your mercy, snatch them from the power of Satan, and redeem them according to your purpose.

CHAPTER ELEVEN

CREATING A CULTURE OF PRAYER AND FASTING

"It is written, 'My house shall be called a house of prayer ...'"
— MATTHEW 21:13

My professors at UVA laid a good foundation in management theory. Though I no longer remember many details from my graduate school studies, in the last decade with Every Nation Philippines, my previous training has again become useful as our ministry has grown. Having read several books on organizational development, I've frequently engaged Ado Bernardo, one of our more knowledgeable Victory pastors on this subject, about how we can apply these principles in leadership development for our movement. One of our recent conversations dwelt on the impact of organizational culture on a church's mission and values.

In our conversation, Ado cited an assertion in Patrick Lencioni's book *The Advantage.* To promote organizational health, a company needs to identify its values and culture. This determines how the management and staff must behave in order to succeed.

Ado explained, "The behavior of the members of an organization is an outworking of their values and culture. The actions and conduct that people see are merely an external manifestation of the culture and values deeply embedded within. People's experiences in church or business establishments, whether good or bad, are determined by the quality of the corporate culture shared by the members of that organization." As Peter Drucker once wrote, "Culture eats strategy for breakfast."

Organizational culture has significant implications on what we do as a church and why we do it. I am learning that some of these lessons apply to creating and sustaining the culture of prayer and fasting. This is another stage in my own leadership journey.

Organizational culture (whether good or bad) is a by-product of leadership.

For a church, creating and sustaining organizational culture is a primary responsibility of the senior pastor and the leadership team. That is an inescapable reality because establishing cultural norms is not only the result of what people do but of which people do it—that is, who takes the active lead. Acts 1:13–15 is the account of what the disciples were doing prior to the outpouring of the Holy Spirit on the Day of Pentecost. All the apostles "with one accord were devoting themselves to prayer, together with the women and Mary the mother of Jesus, and his brothers." Sometime later (perhaps years later), there is the story about the selection of "the seven" to supervise the ministry to widows. The story concludes with the comment from the apostles, "We will devote ourselves to prayer and to the ministry of the word" (Acts 6:1–4).

All the leaders (i.e., the apostles) "with one accord" were intensely devoted to prayer. No matter what leadership style senior pastors employ—whether they empower others by leading from behind the scenes or have a more take-charge personality like the apostle Peter—prayer is never a delegated responsibility. The senior pastor leading the way in personal and corporate prayer reinforces that culture. It sends an unmistakable signal to the congregation.

Creating and perpetuating organizational culture is the product of what church leaders continually, consistently, and intentionally do. In other words, congregations listen to what leaders say but usually determine what they really believe by what the leaders do—the decisions, policies, and procedures they install. Organizational culture is about a history of consistent emphasis and decisions of all kinds that, over time, establish and confirm the real core values. Sometimes, these are in contrast with the published values. In essence, this is how leaders and organizations build culture.

As a leader in the church, I understand what it's like being spiritually drawn and quartered—that is, being pulled in every direction. On any given day, the job of a senior pastor—even of a relatively small congregation—is never really done. There are always more people to meet, more decisions to make, more needs to address. Senior leaders being devoted to prayer and to the ministry of the word (Acts 2:42) is more difficult than most imagine.

Pastors and ministry leaders particularly need your prayers. One of my personal prayers is that the church would pray more for their leaders.

PRAYER FOR CHURCH LEADERS

Lord, I lift our pastors and ministry leaders up to you and ask that you fill and empower them with your Holy Spirit. Give them wisdom on how to manage the unending demands on their time. Give them a peace that surpasses understanding as they minister to those in crisis. Give them guidance and supernatural direction to see the way forward. Protect them from unnecessary distractions that would dominate their time and attention. Bless their families and protect them from the attacks of Satan.

Organizational culture is also the responsibility of each church member.

No matter how devoted the senior leader or the leadership team is to prayer and fasting, organizational cultures are perpetuated by congregations that are willing to follow with a similar, if not greater, burden for prayer. The prevailing culture of intercession in the early church was demonstrated not only by the apostles taking the lead but by how the church responded when faced with crises. The early church as a whole responded the way the first apostles did. As an ongoing practice and at every critical juncture, they repeatedly devoted themselves to prayer. Had the apostles not led the way and modelled this, it is doubtful that the early disciples would have been so devoted to prayer.

PRAYER FOR CHURCH MEMBERS

Holy Spirit, create in me and our congregation a hunger and thirst for your presence. Give us a glimpse of what can be accomplished only through prayer. Restore childlike faith in each of us so that in every challenge we are faced with, we believe that with you, all things are possible. Teach each of us to deny the flesh in order that we may sit in your presence and be transformed into your image. Forgive us for seeking comfort and entertainment in our unrelenting pursuit of things that have no value in light of eternity. Forgive each of us for following you at such a distance and for hanging on so tenaciously to the things of this life.

Organizational culture should be treated as a living thing that bears fruit in every aspect of the church.

When we think of organizational culture, what immediately comes to mind are strategic-planning concepts like mission, vision, and values, or performance metrics like product reliability, customer satisfaction, and brand identification. However, organizational culture (and particularly church culture) is not an object or a sterile concept that is simply adopted or inherited. Emulating the word of God, organizational culture should be "living and active" too (Hebrews 4:12).

There has probably never been a people group with a more defined and enduring culture than the children of Israel. Yet there are no Greek or Hebrew words in the Bible that are translated as "culture." The closest word conveying the idea is translated as "tradition"—that is, social and religious expectations passed down from generation to generation, many of them orally, through storytelling. Though the word "culture" is rarely used in English translations of the Bible, that doesn't mean people of the ancient world were unaware of the concept. It was simply spoken of in an agri-**cultural** or horti-**cultural** context. When Jesus wanted to make a point about the impact of a culture, he said, "The kingdom of heaven is like leaven that a woman took and hid in three measures of flour, till it was all leavened" (Matthew 13:33). When he referred to the effects of a toxic culture, he said, "Beware of the leaven of the Pharisees and Sadducees" (Matthew 16:11). In one way or another, organizational culture (i.e., the culture of leaven) infects and makes an impact on every aspect of our church or ministry.

The noun "culture" is a modern creation from the verb "cultivate." In chapter 4, I commented on the biblical image of God's people as "the vineyard of the LORD" (Isaiah 5:7). An organizational culture that has a positive impact on the vision and values of the church must be tended, watered, and carefully pruned so that it might bear fruit. Carefully managed organizational culture bears increasing abundant fruit and multiplies our impact a hundredfold. In particular, Victory has five long-standing core values: Lordship, evangelism, discipleship, leadership, and family. The reason prayer and fasting are not included in that list is because communion with God is the foundation. It undergirds and empowers every aspect of everything we do.

Lordship—A sense of God's presence in prayer fuels our desire to surrender all.

Evangelism—Communion with God gives rise to a burden for unbelievers.

Discipleship—In the words of Pastor Joey Bonifacio, we understand that "discipleship is relationship" with God and one another.

Leadership—What good would it be for people to go through Victory's discipleship journey and help others follow Jesus without being devoted to prayer? When difficult times come their way, they would wither and scatter like seed landing in shallow soil (Matthew 13:19).

Family—We grow in our faith as part of a church community, from going through *One2One* and joining a Victory group to leading others. We pray for one another, our church, our unsaved friends, and our families with great expectations. "Confess your sins to one another and pray for one another, that you may be healed" (James 5:16).

If a church gets the cultural foundation right, it will affect every aspect of its core values. "Do you not know that a little leaven leavens the whole lump?" (1 Corinthians 5:6).

PRAYER FOR CHURCHES

I pray that your kingdom would come, and your will would be done on earth and in our congregation as it is in heaven. May the culture in our church be aligned with your purpose. Give us grace as a body of believers to be devoted to prayer and the word. Baptize us afresh in your Holy Spirit, that we would be consumed by love for one another and for those who do not know you.

Cultural foundations are subtly planted in future generations of disciples and churches.

Continuing with another application of agri-**culture** and vineyard imagery, Isaiah refers to God's covenant people as "the planting of the LORD," and says that those plants will be "called oaks of righteousness" (Isaiah 61:3). When Pastor Rice and Pastor Steve planted Victory in U-Belt, the "planting of the LORD" was embedded with unique spiritual and cultural

DNA, much of which had been passed down from others. Some of those inherited characteristics were faith, camaraderie, missions, discipleship, and desperate reliance on prayer. My friends and partners in ministry, Ferdie, Jun, and Pastor Steve, have also written books about these.

I hesitate to apply the symbolism of parables and metaphors beyond their intended purpose, but the plain truth is that a small amount of leaven causes the whole lump to rise. What was initially hidden in the dough (Matthew 13:33) eventually permeates and becomes evident. While organizational culture is often more a hidden impartation than an explanation, much of it rides on the leadership team and how intentionally they build the culture. The initial and subsequent church leadership teams have a lot to do with establishing the organizational culture of a church. It's probably easier to get the culture right from the beginning than to change it after many years. Like leaven hidden in the loaf, culture seeps into the foundation of an organization in ways that are initially hard to identify, but eventually become apparent to all.

The apostle Paul wrote in a letter to Timothy, "What you have heard from me in the presence of many witnesses entrust to faithful men, who will be able to teach others also" (2 Timothy 2:2). There are four generations of disciples mentioned in this verse: Paul, Timothy, faithful men who are able to teach, and others. In the same way, we have a responsibility to the next generations. We continue to value prayer, fasting, intercession, and communion with God as we preach the gospel and make disciples. We trust that the broad definition of our organizational culture and core values leaves room for the next generations to have their own encounters with God and stories of kingdom advancement.

The goal is not to replicate a previous empowering of the Spirit by copying how things were done by an older generation. The character of our movement is to continue pressing forward, not be legalistically fixated on the past. We honor and learn from the past, but we don't worship it. We resist the temptation to formalize the culture of prayer by insisting that we should pray a certain way for certain things, for a specific length of time. The last thing we want to do is go back to trusting in a formula to empower us to pray rather than simply trusting in the empowering presence of the Holy Spirit.

PRAYER FOR FUTURE LEADERS

I pray that you raise up new generations of leaders who are filled with your Spirit and devoted to prayer and the ministry of the word (Acts 6:3–4). Give them wisdom to understand that we can accomplish nothing for the kingdom of God without the empowering of your Spirit. I pray that their love would be genuine, and they would abhor what is evil and hold fast to what is good. May they love one another with brotherly affection, outdo one another in showing honor, and not be slothful but fervent in spirit, serving the Lord. I pray they would rejoice in hope, be patient in tribulation, and be constant in prayer (Romans 12:9–12).

Organizational culture (whether good or bad) is a by-product of leadership.

Lord, I lift our pastors and ministry leaders up to you and ask that you fill and empower them with your Holy Spirit. Give them wisdom on how to manage the unending demands on their time. Give them a peace that surpasses understanding as they minister to those in crisis. Give them guidance and supernatural direction to see the way forward. Protect them from unnecessary distractions that would dominate their time and attention. Bless their families and protect them from the attacks of Satan.

Organizational culture is also the responsibility of each church member.

Holy Spirit, create in me and our congregation a hunger and thirst for your presence. Give us a glimpse of what can be accomplished only through prayer. Restore childlike faith in each of us so that in every challenge we are faced with, we believe that with you, all things are possible. Teach each of us to deny the flesh in order that we may sit in your presence and be transformed into your image. Forgive us for seeking comfort and entertainment in our unrelenting pursuit of things that have no value in light of eternity. Forgive each of us for following you at such a distance and for hanging on so tenaciously to the things of this life.

Organizational culture should be treated as a living thing that bears fruit in every aspect of the church.

I pray that your kingdom would come, and your will would be done on earth and in our congregation as it is in heaven. May the culture in our church be aligned with your purpose. Give us grace as a body of believers to be devoted to prayer and the word. Baptize us afresh in your Holy Spirit, that we would be consumed by love for one another and for those who do not know you.

Cultural foundations are subtly planted in future generations of disciples and churches.

I pray that you raise up new generations of leaders who are filled with your Spirit and devoted to prayer and the ministry of the word (Acts 6:3–4). Give them wisdom to understand that we can accomplish nothing for the kingdom of God without the empowering of your Spirit. I pray that their love would be genuine, and they would abhor what is evil and hold fast to what is good. May they love one another with brotherly affection, outdo one another in showing honor, and not be slothful but fervent in spirit, serving the Lord. I pray they would rejoice in hope, be patient in tribulation, and be constant in prayer (Romans 12:9–12).

CHAPTER TWELVE

PRAYER FOR A GREAT AWAKENING

"Behold, the days are coming," declares the LORD, "when the plowman shall overtake the reaper and the treader of grapes him who sows the seed . . ."

—AMOS 9:13

We don't just seek the presence of God for our own lives. We also have a part to play in believing for God's visitation in our community—sowing good seed, cultivating and watering the plants, and harvesting the fruit. We commit to intercession and show compassion and kindness, much like applying fertilizer to promote growth. Be assured, whenever you preach the gospel and invite a person to follow Christ more closely, the Holy Spirit uses God's word to penetrate the deepest and darkest areas of in a person's life—just as Isaiah said it would:

"For as the rain and the snow come down from heaven and do not return there but water the earth, making it bring forth and sprout, giving seed to the sower and bread to the eater, so shall my word be that goes out from my mouth; it shall not return to me empty, but it shall accomplish that which I purpose, and shall succeed in the thing for which I sent it."

—ISAIAH 55:10-11

Growth takes time. No matter how well-rehearsed your gospel presentation, spiritual awakening on the campus or in the community doesn't happen automatically, and rarely as quickly as we would like. No one could empathize more with unsuccessful struggles to bear fruit than the apostle Paul. The opposition and resistance he encountered in almost every city were epic. He escaped Damascus through a window being lowered in a basket (Acts 9:24–25), was stoned and left for dead in Lystra (Acts 14:19), started a riot in Ephesus (Acts 19), was scorned and discounted by the philosophers on Mars Hill (Acts 17), and so on. His efforts often resulted in a relatively small group of believers, surrounded by fanatical opponents.

As Paul wrote to the church in Corinth, "I planted, Apollos watered, but God gave the growth. So neither he who plants nor he who waters is anything, but only God who gives the growth" (1 Corinthians 3:6–7). This suggests that an outpouring of the Spirit and a harvest of new believers is not only a sovereign act of God but the outcome of our co-laboring with Christ through prayer and fasting, gospel demonstration, and gospel proclamation.

There are indeed seasons in which the process of sowing and reaping is not at all slow—more like a movement at light speed. The prophet Amos said, "'Behold, the days are coming,' declares the LORD, 'when the plowman shall overtake the reaper and the treader of grapes him who sows the seed'" (Amos 9:13). The word of the Lord contains a paradox. The seed will bear fruit so rapidly that the planters catch up with the harvesters. In fact, fruit appears supernaturally before it is even planted. That's not just fast, it's a time warp—but that's what happens in a genuine outpouring of the Holy Spirit.

• • •

The promise that "the days are coming" was fulfilled on the day of Pentecost, but in another sense, there have been seasons in which the Holy Spirit has been poured out in much the same way. That was the apostle Peter's observation regarding the remarkable revival at the house of the

Roman centurion, Cornelius. In his report to the other apostles back in Jerusalem, Peter said,

> *"As I began to speak, the Holy Spirit fell on them **just as on us at the beginning**. And I remembered the word of the Lord, how he said, 'John baptized with water, but you will be baptized with the Holy Spirit.' If then God gave the same gift to them as he gave to us when we believed in the Lord Jesus Christ, who was I that I could stand in God's way?"*
>
> — ACTS 11:15–17

In Acts, we see that the outpouring of the Spirit was not a one-time occurrence but something that would happen periodically. During those times of refreshing that come from the presence of the Lord (Acts 3:20), the principles of sowing and reaping are greatly accelerated. You preach the gospel and people respond without delay; you pray for a miracle and it happens almost immediately. There is such an infusion of faith that it seems Christians are easily enabled to believe that all things are possible. This is what happens when the church experiences an outpouring of the Holy Spirit. Those seasons are commonly referred to as revivals or spiritual awakenings. Subsequently, the fruit seems to be ripe for the picking. For example, Philip (not one of the twelve apostles) went down to Samaria to "proclaim to them the Christ."

> *And the crowds with one accord paid attention to what was being said by Philip, when they heard him and saw the signs that he did. For unclean spirits, crying out with a loud voice, came out of many who had them, and many who were paralyzed or lame were healed. So there was much joy in that city.*
>
> — ACTS 8:6–8

There was an extraordinary outpouring of the Spirit in Samaria. Two characteristics of great awakenings are that those most resistant to the gospel become believers and that great leaders emerge. In the Samaritan awakening, even one of the most notorious opponents, Simon the magician, became a believer (Acts 8:9–13). After this, Philip left Samaria to help the Ethiopian eunuch understand the gospel and baptize him in water (Acts 8:26–40). It is generally believed that millions of Ethiopian Orthodox Christians can trace the roots of their faith in Jesus Christ to the Ethiopian eunuch. Philip probably never knew about the impact of this brief encounter. However, 2,000 years later, they're still celebrating Philip's willingness to leave the Samaritan movement and go down the Gaza road.

• • •

My first exposure to a genuine spiritual awakening or outpouring of the Holy Spirit was in the late 1980s as a graduate student at UVA. The campus church I was attending showed a video of a great awakening that took place on the campus of Asbury College in 1970.[1] I was only ten years old in 1970 and twenty-five as a student at UVA. So what may seem like ancient history to college students today had occurred fifteen years earlier when I first saw that video. I had never imagined anything like what I saw in the film clips of students at Asbury's Hughes Auditorium, and it created a burning desire to experience something like that. Almost thirty years later, I found myself enrolled in a Doctor of Ministry program at Asbury Theological Seminary, along with seven other Every Nation pastors and over twenty other graduate students. I don't remember how long it took me to put the two institutions together, but eventually, it occurred to me that the seminary was right across the street from Asbury College. It was like an epiphany, when the hairs on the back of your neck stand at attention. I again felt that sense of God's sovereign plan working its way through my life, that I was being guided by an unseen hand.

Asbury College, with a student population of 1,100 in 1970, was established in 1890 as a Christian college and named after the primary founder of the Methodist church in America, Bishop Francis Asbury. Dr. Dennis Kinlaw (1922–2017), the president of Asbury College from 1968 to 1981, was at a conference in Alberta, Canada, when something very unusual began on the Asbury campus in Kentucky. Arriving at his hotel on Tuesday, February 3, he found that Dr. Custer Reynolds, the academic dean, had left him an emergency message. Kinlaw's blood pressure immediately went up. He called Dean Reynolds, who quickly got to the point.

"It's chapel," he said. "It's not over yet."

"What do you mean, it's not over?" Kinlaw replied, looking at his watch. It was 7:00 p.m. in Wilmore, Kentucky.

Dean Reynolds explained that he had been scheduled to speak at the Asbury College chapel service that morning but instead felt the Holy Spirit's prompting to simply give his testimony. With five minutes remaining in the chapel service, Dr. Reynolds returned to his seat. A philosophy professor sitting in the front row turned to him and said, "God is here. If you give an invitation, there will be a response."

Dr. Reynolds did give an invitation and students did respond in a way that no one could have ever foreseen. The service continued as they responded all that day, into the evening, and throughout the night. The great awakening that began on Tuesday morning on February 3 in Hughes Auditorium continued nonstop, night and day for seven days, the service ending on the following Tuesday.

Dr. Kinlaw recounted, "It spread to campuses, to other churches, and across denominational lines. Most of us were United Methodists, but the revival probably had a larger numerical impact in the Southern Baptist churches. One Asbury student told his story at Southwestern Baptist Seminary and a similar outpouring of the Spirit came upon all those in the classroom."

After watching the videos of what happened at Asbury College, I would be hard pressed for words to adequately describe the event. I could sense the presence of God even then, and would get those same goosebumps and the desire for my own spiritual renewal whenever I reviewed it.[2]

Prayer and Fasting for a Great Awakening

During the revival at Asbury College, a reporter interviewed Dr. Kinlaw over the telephone. The reporter was working on a story about what were, to him, the strange events taking place at the college. Dr. Kinlaw commented on a portion of that conversation.

REPORTER: So, you call this a spontaneous revival?

DR. KINLAW: Yes, that's one way to describe it.

REPORTER: Now, really what you mean is you've had these kinds of things before?

DR. KINLAW: Yes, we have—over a period of years.

REPORTER: What you mean is that you had a group on your campus that said, "We haven't had a spontaneous revival in a long time; we should have one"?

DR. KINLAW: Sir, we have a group of people like that on this campus all the time, but they don't seem to be able to produce it.

REPORTER: Well sir, how do you account for what is happening?

DR. KINLAW: I would suspect that this would be difficult for you, but the only way I know how to explain it is that last Tuesday morning, Jesus walked into Hughes Auditorium . . . and he's been here ever since.

On the one hand, the outpouring of the Spirit at Asbury College in 1970 was a sovereign act of God. Any attempt to remanufacture what God did in a particular place and with a particular group of college students would seem inappropriate—somewhat like the 450 prophets of Baal going through all their hysterics and self-mutilation trying to convince a lifeless idol to call down fire from heaven (1 Kings 18:20–40). What happens more commonly is that zealous Christians try to mimic all the circumstances of a previous move of the Holy Spirit, thinking that doing the identical thing will recreate the same outpouring of love, grace, and power. It is the same appeal against formalism I discussed in the first three chapters—the vain hope that the right form would somehow flip a switch and turn on the power supply. I suspect that future outpourings of the Holy Spirit will take on a different dimension, have a different application, and happen in a different location.

On the other hand, some general preconditions for and characteristics of great awakenings are worth noting—distinctives that were prominent before and during the outpouring of the Spirit at Asbury College.

Pray for the conviction of sin, the humility for confession, and the grace for repentance.

The singular focus was on getting right with God and with one another. Following an informal process, students and faculty members came to the front one by one to confess personal sin, repent tearfully, and dedicate their lives to Christ. This had been going on for four days by the time Dr. Kinlaw returned to the campus from Canada. He went directly to Hughes Auditorium and took a seat at the very back. After about an hour, a student approached him and said, "Dr. Kinlaw, I have to talk to you in private." They went into a downstairs classroom and she began.

"Dr. Kinlaw, I'm a liar," she said. "I lie so much. I don't even know when I'm lying. What do I do?"

The president sat there for a moment or two and finally replied, "Why don't you start with the last person you remember lying to, confess to that person, and ask him or her to forgive you?"

"Oh," she said, "that would kill me!"

Dr. Kinlaw said, "No, it would probably cure you."

Three days later, she came to the president, radiant, and exclaimed, "I'm free!"

"What do you mean you're free?"

"I just confessed and asked forgiveness from my thirty-fourth person. And now I'm free!"

The distinctive characteristic of this particular outpouring of the Spirit was holiness. It was as if the Holy Spirit were shining an intense light on every dark corner of a person's most private life. From the testimonies of those who were there, it seemed that the deep conviction of sin was accompanied by an equally powerful manifestation of God's love and forgiveness.

The emphasis was never upon the gifts of the Spirit, though that would not have been foreign to a historic Wesleyan tradition. There was at least one student who gave a testimony about receiving the baptism of the Holy Spirit. Spiritual awakenings, whether they have many manifestations of spiritual gifts or not, are equally authentic. In this particular outpouring of the Spirit, the emphasis was upon sin, the need for repentance, and repairing relationships with God and with one another. In Every Nation churches around the world, demonstrations of the power of the Holy Spirit in healing, visions, and supernatural visitations have served as confirmations of the gospel. At Asbury College in 1970, it was simply the awesome and overwhelming sense of the presence of God.

". . . And the Lord whom you seek will suddenly come to his temple; and the messenger of the covenant in whom you delight, behold, he is coming, says the LORD of hosts. But who can endure the day of his coming, and who can stand when he appears? For he is like a refiner's fire and like fullers' soap. He will sit as a refiner and purifier of silver, and he will purify the sons of Levi and refine them like gold and silver, and they will bring offerings in righteousness to the LORD."
—MALACHI 3:1–3

PRAYER FOR AN OUTPOURING OF THE SPIRIT

Lord Jesus, manifest your presence in our midst and let the convicting and cleansing power of the Holy Spirit move without restraint among us. Awaken us to the reality of your presence. Purify your people as a refiner's fire and cleanse us as with a launderer's soap.

Pray that the Holy Spirit would reveal our desperate need for redemption and renewal.

In Dr. Kinlaw's mind, there was no question that the acute awareness of their need was one of the chief contributors to the outpouring of the Holy Spirit on the Asbury campus. "We needed it worse than anyone else," he recalled, "and God honors need with his infinite mercy." I don't think the Asbury students needed God's mercy and grace more than anyone else. We all have sinned and fall short of God's glory (Romans 3:23), but this group of students came to realize it. This is not unlike the general sense of desperation among the U-Belt students in the early days of Victory. Without divine intervention and the active empowering of the Holy Spirit, **we could do nothing**. The sense of desperate need was the defining characteristic of the U-Belt outreach, and hopefully of our continuing efforts.

In the weeks and months that followed the 1970 awakening, Asbury students visited campuses and churches all over the United States, and wherever they went, their simple testimony usually sparked a similar awakening. It seemed that the less impressive the student, the more effective an instrument that person became. One student was so shy that she would blush at the mention of her name. She went home over the weekend and on a Sunday spoke in five churches. Dr. Kinlaw said, "If my memory is correct, I think there were 200 people that responded in the churches where she told her story."

The significant impact of that outpouring continues to produce fruit that is still evident to this day. Dr. Robert E. Coleman was a professor of evangelism at Asbury Theological Seminary for twenty-seven years and the author of *The Master Plan of Evangelism*. He also authored a book about the Asbury revival entitled *One Divine Moment*, which included a story about two Asbury College students who went to the University of Tennessee at Martin (UTM) to tell them about Jesus coming to their campus. What followed was an outpouring of the Holy Spirit and a harvest of souls on the UTM campus, including several self-proclaimed notorious unbelievers. Many of the UTM campus leaders became pastors, chaplains, and missionaries. By God's divine providence, one of these leaders, my coauthor, Walter Walker, was sent to Mississippi State University and eventually became the campus pastor of Pastors Rice and Steve.

> ### PRAYER FOR AN OUTPOURING OF THE SPIRIT
>
> *As those who are famished and living in a desert, Lord, we hunger and thirst for your presence. Pour out your Spirit once again on all flesh, that everyone who calls upon the name of the Lord shall be saved (Acts 2:21). Raise up leaders to go into all the world, preaching the gospel and making disciples of all nations.*

The great awakening at Asbury College in 1970 was preceded by a concert of prayer.

Dr. Kinlaw recalled the events that led up to the great awakening:

> We had some students who were interested in prayer. One young lady became deeply concerned for the blessing of God on our campus. So, she gathered a group around her, and they started praying in October before the Holy Spirit came in February. Six students came together in what they called "the great experiment." They covenanted for thirty days to take thirty minutes every morning and spend it in prayer, with the word, writing down what truth they got from the word that they were to obey that day; sharing their faith somewhere in the course of the day; and meeting once a week for those thirty days; and checking up on each other to see that each one had done his disciplines that week.
>
> At the end of that thirty days, each one of those six picked up five people. Now there were six groups of six getting up every morning for thirty minutes extra to pray and spend time with God. . . . On the 31st of January, they led the chapel service with thirty-six of them on the platform, sharing what the great experiment had done for them. There was a commitment slip on every seat in the

auditorium, inviting every student to commit himself to become a part of a group of six, who would for thirty days engage in this experiment. That was on Saturday, the 31st of January. In some ways that was the most impressive chapel I think I had ever seen at Asbury. Students sharing what time with God had done for them. That was on the 31st of January. The next chapel was Tuesday, the 3rd of February.

Now, in addition to this, the young lady who I told you about and her group started having nightly prayer meetings. They were praying for God to come, and when they would finish a prayer meeting, they'd look at each other and say, "Do you think he'll come today?"

At one point they organized an all-night prayer meeting in Hughes Auditorium where a large group of students gathered around the altar to pray for their campus. Around 2:30 a.m., they stood around the altar holding hands, and said, "That's enough, he's coming." And they went home and went to bed.[2]

Students testified later that God had told them, "It's going to happen tomorrow."

The next day was the chapel service on Tuesday, February 3.

PRAYER FOR AN OUTPOURING OF THE SPIRIT

Come, Lord Jesus! Visit us with the power of your presence. Grant that your servants continue to speak your word with all boldness, while you stretch out your hand to heal, and signs and wonders are performed through the name of your holy servant Jesus (Acts 4:29–30).

Pray for the conviction of sin, the humility for confession, and the grace for repentance.

Lord Jesus, manifest your presence in our midst and let the convicting and cleansing power of the Holy Spirit move without restraint among us. Awaken us to the reality of your presence. Purify your people as a refiner's fire and cleanse us as with a launderer's soap (Malachi 3:2).

Pray that the Holy Spirit would reveal our desperate need for redemption and renewal.

As those who are famished and living in a desert, Lord, we hunger and thirst for your presence. Pour out your Spirit once again on all flesh, that everyone who calls upon the name of the Lord shall be saved (Acts 2:21). Raise up leaders to go into all the world, preaching the gospel and making disciples of all nations.

The great awakening at Asbury College in 1970 was preceded by a concert of prayer.

Come, Lord Jesus! Visit us with the power of your presence. Grant that your servants continue to speak your word with all boldness, while you stretch out your hand to heal, and signs and wonders are performed through the name of your holy servant Jesus (Acts 4:29–30).

AFTERWORD

"O LORD God of heaven, the great and awesome God who keeps covenant and steadfast love with those who love him and keep his commandments, let your ear be attentive and your eyes open, to hear the prayer of your servant that I now pray before you day and night . . ."

—NEHEMIAH 1:5–6

At the request of Pastor Steve, I began working with Bishop Ferdie, Pastor Jun, and Walter on this account of my spiritual journey and the essential role of prayer in Victory's growth over the last thirty-seven years. There have been many prophetic utterances on what the Holy Spirit is saying to the church and how we are to move forward into the future in the wake of COVID-19. Though Walter is quick to deny any prophetic gifting, he may have said it best: "If there is anything redemptive that would come out of this pandemic, it would be a genuine movement of Spirit-empowered prayer and crying out to God."

• • •

The story of my commitment to deeper fellowship with God and to prayer has really been a progressive journey. It began as a gradual realization of the power of my mother's intercession for me, followed years later by an understanding that relying on a particular pattern for prayer had little sustaining power. Over time I learned that Spirit-empowered discipline comes from an ongoing communion with God. I began cultivating spiritual disciplines to honor the indwelling presence of the Spirit in my life. You might say that I've come full circle with regard to spiritual disciplines—to what Richard Foster, the author of *Celebration of Discipline*, refers to as "holy habits." But a circle would put me right back where I was thirty years ago in my prayer life. I see it more as a long upward journey—like an ascending spiral staircase. As I endeavor to keep moving forward, I am learning that spiritual transformation comes from the sanctifying work of the Holy Spirit and his empowering presence—not from summoning up the determination to overcome the temptations of fleshly desires. As Brother Lawrence prayed when contemplating his faults and momentary lapses in spiritual disciplines, "Lord, unless you change me, I will always be this way."

This book was never meant to be a definitive treatise on every aspect of prayer, only on the aspects I've begun to learn, reaffirming what the apostle Paul wrote: "Now we see in a mirror dimly, but then face to face. Now I know in part; then I shall know fully, even as I have been fully known" (1 Corinthians 13:12).

Moving Right Along

I completed my doctoral studies at Asbury Theological Seminary in 2019. It was a rich, rewarding, and quite tedious learning experience. The distance-learning program included numerous days of intense study on the Kentucky campus. After graduation, I began checking things off my bucket list that I felt called to accomplish. I returned to a full-time focus on my responsibilities as a member of the Victory Bishops Council, which provides spiritual leadership for our churches in the Philippines. One of the most important of those roles is leading the way in the ministry of intercession. Not that I am more frequent, more effective, or more passionate in prayer than others. That is far from being the case. So, you might say that I am one of the prayer organizers—but that's probably not accurate either. I see evidence every day that the Holy Spirit is inspiring and empowering more intercession than I could ever hope to organize. Maybe it's best to simply say that I continued to fellowship with God in prayer and encouraged others to join me.

AFTERWORD

. . .

At UVA, Pastors Mark and Stephen introduced me to Noah Webster's original 1828 *Dictionary of the English Language*. Words in that edition were generally defined in ways consistent with a biblical worldview and often-used passages from the Bible as examples of how the words could be used in sentences. There was one definition I thought to be quite profound. The word "seminary" was defined as:

SEM'INARY, *noun* [Latin seminarium, from semen, seed; semino, to sow.] A seed-plant; ground where seed is sown for producing plants for transplantation; a nursery; as, to transplant trees from a seminary.

The purpose of a good seminary is to be able to transplant leaders and churches all over the world with its cultural and spiritual DNA intact.

My new assignment as the Dean of Spiritual Life of the Every Nation Seminary is, once again, something that I had not planned. While prayer and fasting, intercession, and spiritual disciplines are not always highlighted as crucial elements of seminary education, this is what I am tasked to weave into the theological training of our students. The cultural and spiritual DNA of our church demands that intercession and communion with God vitalize every aspect of what we do—including academic and theological studies. For this reason, my goal is not only to equip our graduate students as preachers and teachers of God's word but also to emphasize the generative power of prayer in their ministries. As the seminary continues to grow and develop more leaders, my faith is that there will be no shortage of intercessory prayer that will continue to bear fruit in every nation.

REFERENCES

Chapter 2: Big on Form, Low on Power

1. Larry Lea, *Could You Not Tarry One Hour?: Learning the Joy of Prayer* (Charisma Book Group, 1987).

2. Darren Whitehead, "As For Me & My House - April 26," Church of the City, filmed April 26, 2021 in Franklin, TN, https://cotc.com/messages/?sapurl=Lys3MDQ2L2xiL2ipLytxeT-JwejJ6P2VtYmVkPXRydWU=.

Chapter 3: Radical Simplicity

3. St. Albert, "The 'Primitive' Rule of the Order of the Blessed Virgin Mary of Mount Carmel," Discalced Carmel, accessed June 24, 2021, https://discalcedcarmel.org/our-carmelite-spirituality/the-rule-of-st-albert/.

4. Marianne Bernhard, "Maria von Trapp Talks About Family, Convent," *The Washington Post*, August 29, 1980.

5. Joan Gearin, "Movie vs. Reality: The Real Story of the Von Trapp Family Prologue Magazine," *Prologue Magazine*, Winter 2005.

6. Comments attributed to Lawrence of the Resurrection are derived from those conversations with Father Beaufort and his letters to Reverend Mother N, as translated from the original French and published under the title *The Practice of the Presence of God: The Best Rule of a Holy Life* (New York: Fleming H. Revell, 2011), Kindle edition.

Chapter 4: Honoring the Presence

7. Richard J. Foster, *Freedom of Simplicity* (New York: HarperCollins Publishers, 1981), 7–8.

8. Sam Keen in Amy E. Spaulding, *The Wisdom of Storytelling in an Information Age: A Collection of Talks* (London: Scarecrow Press, 2004), 112.

9. Peter Thomas Rohrbach, *Conversation with Christ: The Teaching of St. Teresa of Avila About Personal Prayer* (London: Aeterna Press, 2016), in "Carmelite spirituality and the practice of mental prayer," Blogspot, posted January 1, 2006, https://floscarmelivitisflorigera.blogspot.com/2006/01/general-preparation-for-meditation.html.

Chapter 5: Corporate Prayer

10. Steve Murrell, *WikiChurch: Making Discipleship Engaging, Empowering, and Viral* (Lake Mary: Charisma House, 2011), 19.

11. Jun Escosar, *A Bible and a Passport: Obeying the Call to Make Disciples in Every Nation* (Manila: Every Nation Leadership Institute, 2019).

12. Wikipedia, s.v. "Jeremiah Lanphier," accessed June 24, 2021, https://en.wikipedia.org/wiki/Jeremiah_Lanphier.

13. A fuller account of the Great Experiment at Asbury College is given in chapter 12: Prayer for a Great Awakening.

Chapter 6: Praying and Planting

14. Murrell, *WikiChurch*, 43.

15. Escosar, *A Bible and a Passport*, 68.

16. Murrell, *WikiChurch*, 82–83.

Chapter 7: Victory Quezon City

17. Quezon City is the largest city in Metro Manila in terms of land area. As Victory continued to expand, we realized the need for planting several congregations in that city. To make room for this, we decided to change the name of the Victory church in Quezon City to Victory Katipunan. Katipunan Avenue is the main thoroughfare running through the three university campuses and

where our church facility is located. Katipunan refers to a revolutionary society founded in 1892 by anti-colonialist Filipinos who fought for independence from Spain. By faith, we are believing for a spiritual revolution to take place among the students on these campuses. We now have several Victory congregations in Quezon City, with others planned for the future.

Chapter 8: The Role of the Spirit in Prayer

18. Escosar, *A Bible and a Passport*, 143–144.

Chapter 9: Standing in the Gap

19. Dutch Sheets, *Intercessory Prayer: How God Can Use Your Prayers to Move Heaven and Earth* (Minneapolis, MN: Bethany House, 1996).

20. Jonathan Edwards, *Freedom of the Will* (Mineola: Dover Publications, 2012; first published 1754).

Chapter 10: Deliberate Approach to Intercession

21. Steve Murrell and William Murrell, *The Multiplication Challenge* (Lake Mary: Creation House, 2016).

Chapter 12: Prayer for a Great Awakening

22. There are numerous videos of the Asbury revival in 1970, including this one: "A Revival Account: Asbury 1970," at https://youtu.be/7qOqitIKUNs.

23. Dr. Dennis Kinlaw in "A Revival Account: Asbury 1970," YouTube.com, uploaded July 21, 2008, https://youtu.be/7qOqitIKUNs.